LETTER TO POETRY

LETTER TO POETRY

followed by replies

TOM MANDEL

Geben dir meine Schriften nur Anlass, Dich mit einem hohlen Gespenst von Verstehen und Nichtverstehen herumzuschlagen, so lege sie noch beiseite.

> — Friedrich Schlegel
> (from a letter to Schleiermacher)

chax
2022

ISBN 978-1-946104-30-4

Library of Congress Control Number: 2021945354

Chax Press
1517 N Wilmot Rd no. 264
Tucson Arizona 85712-4410

Chax Press books are supported in part by individual
donors and by sales of books. Please visit *https://chax.
org/membership-support/* if you would like to contribute
to our mission to make an impact on the literature and
culture of our time.

From the author:
I am grateful to the editors of *Access Press, Across the
Margin, Elderly,* and *VLAK,* print & online journals where
earlier versions of some of these works appeared.

As well, some of these works first appeared as *Partial Wave
Form,* a chapbook in the Ink series published in France by
Alain Cressan, to whom I am grateful as well.

for Beth Joselow

I who thought to be no more than one

Found you instead to dote upon

CONTENTS

Preface: Letter to Poetry

Dear Poetry,

Having found your address early and by accident, I've been writing you most of my life. Yet until now I haven't thanked you for your replies, perhaps because at first I was so surprised to receive them, perhaps because I still am.

I don't fool myself that you've been impatient for my gratitude. Plenty of attention comes your way these days. You may find much of it burdensome, including this note. Still, I'm grateful: I can't imagine what I'd have done all these years without you.

Common sense tells me to close this note here. But, I ask your indulgence instead, as I recount a conversation I had with our mutual friend Harry Mathews some years ago as we sat on his backyard patio drinking wine and chatting in the late afternoon sun of Key West. Harry handed me a newly-published book of his poems, remarking that to compose it, "I had to teach myself to write poetry all over again."

I found these words puzzling & objected that, although better known for his novels, he'd been a poet the whole of his writing life. Yet, he replied, the poems he'd written over the last few decades had

13

been Oulipian. It was the traditional *craft* of verse he'd needed to relearn to write this new volume.

I continued to object. But the sun descends quickly in those parts. Evening was soon upon us.

Though we never had occasion to return to the subject, Harry's remark stayed with me. As I rehearsed his words in memory, however, two of them swapped places, & I seemed to hear him say, "I had to teach myself to write all poetry over again," a notion which is either ridiculous or meaningless or both.

Yet, it was in this altered version that Harry's words left their mark on me. Beginning a project some weeks later, I found myself writing a few poems which seemed determined to revisit (& in some measure to *revise* as well) distant days & ways from the history of poetry.

It goes without saying that I can't saddle our friend with any responsibility for these odd works. I had no choice. The muse may be a fiction, but we obey her all the same.

Nor should you, or anyone, read these remarks as evincing any impatience with the term *avant-garde*, its shallow teleology, its metaphoric militarism, the air of self-praise that so often marks its use. In this era of an unopposed, pre-canonized & altogether automatic "(p)reproduction of the new," such a label can only be viewed as parodic.

Dear poetry, I hope the preceding paragraph did not offend you! If so, please erase it from your record & mine.

As to the pages that follow, I am able to justify every word, syllable, phoneme & even letter shape found upon them. As who would know better than you.

Thanks again; don't abandon me!

Tom

Remember the Tune

What Matter Does Doesn't

On-off-on the sensor array
Touches palm to palm
While time looks away

There's nothing new to see
No one's left but we
Who dance here hand to hand

Must turn the other cheek
To cheek as face to face
We live from day to day

After Georges Perec

Depressing these utopias
That leave no room for chance

But sort all to an order
Difference won't abide

No habitation in taxonomy
For miscellanies no grant

Nor with all else in position
May any old thing slink

Back to its usual any old place
There's nowhere left to hide

After Novalis

Conversation is an error to admire
        Truth in writing or speech
A play on words for the sake of
        Mad notions people inspire.

Using your gift for mathematics
        Show us the price we pay
Letters to rub shoulders in short-
        Lived dalliance with those

To whom we serve these arrays
        Of ungrasped matters, causing
Distant mirrors that gaze upon us
        From other worlds to break

Into peals of uncontrolled laughter
        At the words people employ
The moment we begin to speak
        Out loud in the name of things

I Was Reminded

What's best about a hand
gives you ways to use it

as best about a handle turns
on what you use it for.

So do hand or handle wind
into all we learn

along the path that links mind
to "is" & "tell" & "fall"

until, ever the optimist, we
place a bet on thought

(but with a pessimist's hedge
on time that unlike

thought parts before a path
nears it) singing:

happy, fly, like thee to die
are we whose gestures

precarious may brush thee
from the day yet

some may prefer (all the
same) to pause such

play, hearing a hand or
wing fold, to drop

shapes taken in order that
one object may touch

another & lacking quest
or other purpose cause

a hand to fall away
to slip from its handle.

Grand Piano Dialogues

1. with Kit Robinson

KIT: According to Victor Shklovsky, in order to write about love one must write about everything not about love.

TOM: Desire is that, whatever, wanting to be satisfied. There is no desire without objectification. I see the pigeon on a city street; he courts a crack in the sidewalk.

KIT: As one story leads to the next, plots & subplots hinging & depending from one another in an elaboration of imaginary relationships, events cascade across time until suddenly the man's hand jerks forward & knocks over a glass of wine, staining the white tablecloth.

TOM: You were reading Shklovsky, I was reading Bataille.

KIT: Did you think money grew on trees?

TOM: I think history is a series of repetitions, each of

which we nonetheless greet with surprise, convinced somehow, in the face of the same thing over & over, that something new has happened.

KIT: Benjamin wrote of the Jewish tradition that each moment may signify the arrival of the Messiah, so that history is shot through with chips of messianic time.

TOM: We cannot shed the light that falls on us.

KIT: I think back a quarter century, Tom, when a quarter was worth something, well, not really, when the century was twentieth, & upside down just looked like right side up to us.

TOM: Literature is a great sailing ship. We writers imagine ourselves manning her sails or as the wind which fills them. But we are waves she cuts across, no more.

KIT: & who, just exactly, is speaking?

TOM: Facts are fractal. There can be no such "movement" as LANGUAGE POETRY.

2. *with Lyn Hejinian*

TOM: It's possible to have a lot of confidence, even to be effective in the world, without much sense of purpose.

LYN: Those are the things we can work with, seeing them as precisely that—what one has to work with.

TOM: Political thought interrupts other thinking.

LYN: Imagination is turned to the present; it is the present moment that wants expanding.

TOM: The walls of Fred Hampton's apartment were marked by hundreds of bullet holes. We walked on boards that lay across puddles of blood.

LYN: The stiff geometric youngster of suicide seems to have bartered away something in exchange for the beauty of heroism.

TOM: Each of us knows the answer in advance; to think is to be an ideologist.

LYN: One imagines one has somehow been misled, taken, or gotten lost.

TOM: Taxonomy is simple, transparent; it only shows itself to reward your attention.

LYN: The epic is monumental; the saga is long, a testimony to powerlessness.

TOM: The older I get, I need to lean in close to read the writing on the wall.

LYN: A gust is already blowing aside the curtain over the bed.

TOM: This is how I understand the phrase "the person who makes," who arises in the identification, as a source of attraction, an occasion for desire, someone to love.

LYN: The characters include "Vice President Boynton, who kicks chairs when he gets mad & hopes to do a swan dive into your conscience."

TOM: Famously, after a symphonic work ends, the hall reverberates with silence. Then there is applause.

LYN: & then she told her mother, "Mother, take him home & make him rest."

Circular Labors

I wander happily
a world where others

travel too as a rising
breeze puts out the

blaze someone's sure
to claim I ignited

when in pain I dropped
my candle, crying

"Why this repeated
impact of collections

& my forehead?" If
memory inquires what

collisions serve, I
hope you will agree?

Wearing my blindfold
I strolled my library's

perimeter (to the
soundtrack I'd chosen

Marvin Gaye's tenor
croon; I hope you

approve) when be-
hind covert eyes

heat engulfing my
step I hit the shelf

the walk taken to
unwind my clocks

& time my domin-
ion's geometry, this

despite the advice
of so many to wind

them instead (but
none could tell me

how). Time's arrow
whatever might

fade when spoken
falls in the heart of

every herd the same
voices deny, I'll

never know why.
For time may pass

notice when the
flame subsides to

quiet the fuss in
a motion faint as

a second hand's minus-
cule, trembling hop

how forlorn! that
one time was the

source of its promise.
Fainter yet follows

an instant of repose
to ready repetition

the only trick it knows.
Fiery the day (don't

deny it!) when our
premises may reprove

what no memory
will ever improve: for

this I still can prove:
a molehill aflame

burns it down: a
famous mountain town.

Shaped All Ways

The grass dissolves beneath your feet
You cast your glance along the street

Shop signs start to rust
Minds compact to dust

You feel tomorrow's heat
Around the corner you retreat

To render the future just
The wind whips up a little gust

Strange triumphs follow defeat
The past is gone, it can't be beat

Spinoza taught you whom to trust
Just like Sextus Empiricus

It's only you I want to meet.

Cubical Bird Call

Ready, flee, aim!
in each encounter
sorrow's fraction

A sensual thing
on the brink of joy
speaks of obligation.

The mail arrives
in a cigar box
when a child &

Spring cause this
wonder: "life" as
"simple" advice.

Each letter says
"put me first," for
whatever lives is

dead right before
any coming yester-
day, while minutes

jar slightly in our
captivity. The boss
of spirit will fire

the boss of law in
my jealous dream
of desire. There's

nothing in the still
now but March mud
while, unrequited

even entropy loses
so tenderly does a
lit match play back

cruelty recalled that
the winner shifts
remembered cruelty

a cunning moment
when rare game
comes a-running as

change rises. What
is it to sit back
down? Entropy

against a co-pay?
Gravity dances on
this path; they say

even Proust fell:
one time for a biker
once for a hitchhiker.

Remember the Tune

While I sketch out extra decades
I'll never need you read this page

of missing words each time you drive
the perfect circle of my cage.

Rattle my chains! Upend my tomb!
Components ablaze upon

the curve of God's cryptography
I believe I'll dust my broom.

Every time I look backstage
history takes me back a page

to where paralyzed constants await
revisions that never arrive.

Polynomials rise & fall so fast
you're afraid to teach one thing

about a dozen of the other.
On the day that you return

your last advanced decree
I believe I'll dust my broom.

I play to win. I want to hear
& instantly to care unless

(postponing our collapse) we meet
tomorrow on the corner where

folding your world inside my past
I believe I'll dust my broom.

My interest mounts then halts my pen
before the paper's ruined again.

I'll need some time to take back all
the lies I'm done telling. Dogs may

play me, & subtle human craft works too
yet no replacement ever proves

quite the needle for my groove.
While cat & dog use cod & tag

to sketch out all-new standards
I believe I'll dust my broom.

Missing at a moment's notice
I'm ready to get startled on

a scale of one to ten from none
to when the middleman has breached

our walls & put the pressure on.
I'll always remember the tune.

The dish ran away with the spoon.
I believe I'll dust my broom.

The margin that might tilt this plain
rend my chain, or track the laps

I swim to relax must lapse past
human scale. It's the original of you

I want in my zoo To reach my room
outside the wire, you climb through gloom

you do not tire. Once we depart the womb
I believe I'll dust my broom.

On our trip back to the border
I pointed out a troubled sieve

you'd woven on the loom we left
behind our first time through.

Even the chain of stars that go
BOOM! someone must choose to discard.

I have in mind to bet the farm
but not on that, nor buy it for

that either. Before you try to stop me
I believe I'll dust my broom.

Once upon a time an algorithm
deep in the woods began to crawl

the intellectual property that flourished
unimplemented on the forest floor

until at last it grew to be
your signature. With much to tell

before time fell, night passed quickly
then didn't pass at all. Your patents are

all painted out; I'm done with you.
I believe I'll dust my broom.

As if conversing with my thoughts
some feebler or more strenuous other

by magic might arise
I for whom to live is to think

don't furnish my soul but shape it.
It's one thing to be lost they say

to vanish another: the rarities
I longed for once are useless now:

my banished vocation has been revived.
I believe I'll dust my broom.

Broken Circle Takedowns

How Relaxing

To see more of me lately
What another might miss

Or in case you do, my
"Good old used to be"

Routine has burst aflame
In the kitchen gadget aisle

So this time be clever
It might be now or never

To sing me those "back
In no time" blues.

Broken Circle Takedowns

When token circle breakdowns cause
Fault lines to cross cloud nine

Your words begin to haunt me like
Last year's big idea

Recounted all wrong tomorrow.
"It's hard to live where one

Was happy once." Pavese's words
Ring true, but do they

Matter? Nowadays, after all
No one lives anywhere

Not even for a little while.
I've said it many times

What irony would undermine
First it must assert:

I started out to waste my time
Maybe now I have outlived it.

Bitter Delicious

Nouns display yearning
fire best seen in the sun

whose verb moves the real
car you love, you spend

lit up new each morning
to stay in place, then take off

at the same time polishing
put out again each night

until finally turning to a subject
not left from the day before

to read "I was absent that day"
old man, are you proud of years

that science altered, belief itself
pulled apart by grammar

though difficult to locate
whatever page she recalls

we soon learn again
who do not cease expecting tomorrow

it, oil always on our hands
which category brings it near

to see an arc again above her
a thought of her death now long

dirt suspended in it
whom I liked so well despite

is to know those years are gone
in *Corvus* where Anselm cribs

like false quotes of the Buddha
leave no residue on its wheel

if not for anyone he said she was
on refrigerator magnets

we too are born as new
with gloves on when we drive

so she would have you think
again tomorrow, or we hope

. . . what's left began today . . .
all over the Internet, no one

that the sun really circles us
Palladas, *. . . each morning we are . . .*

who was as the writing made her
what persons made them up may care

for what was? What might have been?
to bury itself in the horizon

then standing back admire the work
of a meditation teacher. His name is Jack

. . . remains . . .
appear, & was! Truly!

Kornfield (& psychotherapist) his
will not return tomorrow

constant, avid motion, sexual
bons mots imagined from the Buddha's mouth

adventurer also appeared as child
. . . born again / of yesterday nothing . . .

how useless the remark! What to make of
night left as if to test one's patience

. . . we do today what matters most . . .
jump in the car; drive our course

fervent for all that will not return
time was invented to track the sun

Back in No Time Blues

a.

They say that I'm not humble
        start to talk I'm never through

They say I'm a fool for a rumble
        like to roll, pitch & screw

They don't care do I fall do I stumble
        just turn the glue to dew

They holler "cease thy mumble
        insert beast within zoo!"

2.

A woman you once knew
        took little thought for what you'd do

Perhaps you called her by my name
        she chose to love you just the same

Z.

When the clock comes up at midnight
      one hand false & neither true

Caressed by the moonlight
      someone may paddle my canoe

They say whiskey runs this river
      it's a barrelhouse for two

& that the all-night train from nowhere
      will get no one next to you

The Writing on the Wall Is Waiting at Your Door

Within the precincts of an imagined world
Stolen ideas arise

From monuments of philosophy
Each word recalls

A single mind, each rose its only
Gardener.

A Monument Obscures the Scene of the Crime

i.
Time's a mixed bag
of short rations.

Any day long enough
will outlast night.

The rectangle on your left holds an image of the suspect
in our case; like her victim she is dead, or perhaps one
should add, "therefore"; or (if instead she is holding her
breath, & that after only a few moments to prepare—no
doubt unsatisfactorily, so that too little time may pass for
a camera to capture the effort it costs) we should grant
instead—not with reluctance but enthusiastically—primacy
to this illusion, which is after all the vector along which the
aforementioned rectangle means to propel us.

ii.
To stymie its pattern
hold your palm up to time

Our proposed 60-second spot depicts an awkward individual,
male, emerging from under a rock (his home, as will be
made obvious by shot details) to save up to 25 percent. The
intention to amuse, also to convince, though perhaps not on

*its own but in combination with a soon-to-be-aired spot in
which we are seated at the side of a woman, fur at her throat,
eyes closed, not at all ill at ease, as she drives a well-known
but pointless, roundabout route (to include a number of
turns, both left & right) to the unnamed town's train station,
our elite audience may be expected to grasp. Arrived at the
station she greets the advance party. As if by chance, but
this is anything but coincidental, they are forty plus eight
in number, as are the Preludes & Fugues of Bach's* Well-
Tempered Clavier, *which we hear on the soundtrack."* (a
marginal note reads: "but not the whole thing! Please
clarify in next draft")

*Weary, of his state but also of his name, a video engineer
rises from his workstation & removes the circumaural
Beyerdynamic studio cans that have powered his day of
contemplation & judgment, a simple gesture which reinforces
his intimate relationship with them, his right to have donned
them, & the right they grant him to take in, as a singularity
but also as a myriad, a soundscape another has created &
to exhibit a seemingly improvisational ease with whatever
comes next in the score, so that each fall of finger on control
key unrolls tones that grant to none the scope to unravel.*

*The director lives to see depicted the noble but tragic (though
inevitable) triumph of crow-madman over neon-dirt-hall-
cousin with whom circumstance, or else chance (shaped in
the final screenwriters' plot conference), has forced a contest.*

A kind of bipartisan diffidence, not an absence of desire
but an intentional glance away from anything that might
provoke desire, seems to be one effect of the salutary climate
hereabouts. Let me say right away that for this thing we are
prepared to provide an altogether different soundtrack, maybe
something delicate that can absorb blood as well as shed it?
As needed?

iii.
Up drives the black Cadillac
that's come to take me back

To where I first heard the tone
of Zen inside a koan

When (payday come & gone)
You swore that I alone

Would be the one to own
the brand-new stick-built home

You showed me on your phone
while counting out my loan.

But wrenchmen on the dome
prised up the royal throne.

The piece I meant to hone
in polystyrene foam

Time cradled like a bone
Howlin' Wolf might bemoan

Whose well-known, down-home groan
would prove I was no clone

But a voice time had sewn
by choice inside this zone

Instead was turned to stone
& my cover was blown.

iv.
While I stretched out in the back
Of that limo Cadillac

With a pencil from my purse
On the coffin in that hearse

You wrote a love note to my nurse.
But what was even worse

To lock me in your curse
You erased my final verse

The one I'd scribbled inside its lid.
That was the first thing that you did.

v.

When the Cadillac stopped at the light
I saw the driver & took fright
She brought to mind that awful night

A night that felt like leather
The night we spent together

That night I made my first mistake
I put my holster in the toaster
I tried to drown it in the lake

vi.

From above, a camera mounted on our newsbreak helicopter zooms in on the SUV slowly, until it fills the frame. Inverted, the vehicle lays at a precarious angle, all its weight on its partially collapsed roof, its twisted unibody splayed from bottom left to top right of our screen above a bright red banner across which four-word phrases in yellow scroll smoothly from right to left, succeeding one another at a constant pace until their motion stops & we read: "Call This Number Now."

Relic Taste

Surprises last forever
Unknown folds of dawn
A tyrant's letter follows
Its words stare down

A word lasts forever
Dawn unfolds letters
Unknown numbers follow
The tyrant stares down

The tyrant lasts forever
A letter folds surprises
Words unknown follow
Dawn stares down

Dawn lasts forever
Surprises fold a word
Unknown tyrants follow
The letter stares down

The letter lasts forever
Words fold tyrants
An unknown follows dawn
Numbers stare down

Numbers last forever
The unknown tyrant folds
A letter follows words
Surprises stare down

Red Tux

A whiskey in one hand in the other a pill
Through the windshield of my Coupe de Ville
I watch as you fill the future with lies.
In a black mohair suit, in a very small size
With tapered trousers I stare from the past
& whisper, "Those lies are all that will last
Of the perpetual motion despairing machine
I've made of your words. It reads like a dream."

For forty nights & their following days
I will think of you & practice your ways.
I will roll my Caddy over your grave to feel
Dirt of the past go black beneath my wheel
The wheel that rolls on my old Coupe de Ville.
Though they scoff, "No you won't," you know I will.

Let None Interfere

I hang around where nothing inheres
bouncing my Spaldeen off a stoop.

To move forward I lift the weight
from my back foot & fall down.

Are you still so smart? Still derive
pleasure from beneath the floor?

After decades of irony left me
exhausted I set my burden down

to ask but found no answer & so
opened this shop where I sell what

I can & what I can't I can to keep
on hand for the day when, fresh stuff

gone, I'm left clinging to the fringes
of my skill in this tent city they say

two tribes founded the day a wrong
turn swept their clans to our misread

address & with them a mingled
multitude whose names got on the

signup list mistakenly when someone
yelled "All those who are ready to

depart this place, please raise a hand"
& hearing "parse this phrase" we did.

Ouroboros

My Chinese teacher in Paris whispered
       "Make your decision & make it quick
Call it a prediction to make it stick
       for time is the bark to thicken your tree."

"But most men are con men," I exclaimed.
       "Are not you one too?"
"Before it's been bent three times," he explained
       "no word renders true."

"The path seems too narrow!" I cried.
       "Not at all," he replied.
          "The roadway is wide."

"There's a knot in my rope," I lied.
       "From here," he sighed,
          "it looks untied."

RFC 1+1: Rebirth of the Internet

Over fallow fields gazed on from his wheel
The morning begins in mist & chill,
Yet, though lightning flashes as he drives
The predicted rainfall never arrives.

Later that day upon his hotel room
Curtain a print of leaves in autumn
Contradicts the sunny June weather.
The afternoon fills with warmth & pleasure.

Must each rise be begotten by a fall?
No, he's simply run into the wall
While seeking something useful to say
That like the rain will not arrive today.

He doesn't imagine he can play God
He's a better Falstaff, which (though odd)
Helps to explain why once in a while
He muses on weather in sing-song style.

Remind Me

On Solidarity Street the traffic cop
routes most cars around the bend. *Get thee
behind me methodology,* I hear
his whistle sing, a token made to send

means to the end of midwinter, when
spring, neither behind nor ahead,
resembles a fence whose gaps inscribe
parabolae—games to play that won't

dismay the mental surface of a driver
idling in the vicinity of pleasure's
weightless white dividing lines

to wonder what the cop must think:
"Maybe more hot air would make it
safe to cross the brink of this thin ice?"

A Perfeck Attact

In its first moments
A pencil aims to travel

Along a list of routes
Excited, morose maps

Nature means to draw
For one's kind review

According well with
Yours (i.e., his) between

A scratch the small
Dog must have left

& the love line (if
It's still called that)

At rest upon the palm
A capsule dissolves

Or drops. I had a
Glimpse moments

Ago (as if entry on
A list would ease

Search or leave us
Capsules, simple

Consolation fallen
Beneath metaphor

Vintage, an original
Holiday present some-

One had in find to
Fix on tomorrow).

But, no, swallowed
Surely, then forgotten

Like a noun no longer
Used on that occasion

But which one comes
Upon from time to

Time in a thrift store
Bin, thrown among

Disused guides to
Life as the hodge-

Podge of harmless
Hobbies it often is.

A map odd weather
Renders possible will

Lead the few friends
Still morose away

From my path.
Fallen, swallowed

To mimic another's
Nature & become

(As may the name
On an old map of

A town one hasn't
Visited, folded &

Refolded in use)
Invisible: yet off

They go traveling
Far too from who

Knows where they
Started or were born

For many die else-
Where, yet death is

So often left off a
Map: as a capsule

Drops to the floor
Stops or else rolls

Out the door. No –
There it is! Not a

Capsule, a grape,
its torn skin bright

With indented form,
Escaped no more.

Though buying a
Grape won't break

The bank, don't drop
Its stem: for things

That fall, like those
That stall, may cause

The tallest tale to veer
Into a vale of tears.

Frankie & Johnny
Songs, salvos, psalms & alarms

Frankie & Johnny

Frankie felt the darkness surround him as a child
Johnny flipped a light switch on & off & smiled

Frankie speaks out loud, "It's coming on for night"
Johnny shapes the silence to fit around him tight

Frankie flies an all-day plane
Johnny rides the bullet train

Frankie sees the pharmacist shoot him for the flu
Johnny's in a storefront to choose a new tattoo

Frankie's head is shaking, "This is a mean old world"
Johnny reads a magazine as he gets his hair recurled

Frankie is strong in this & every room
Johnny spreads his arms to bring the temple doom

Frankie pound for pound turns things around
Johnny by the minute hammers on the ground

Frankie writes hexameter way inside his head
Johnny bounces a ball back to where it led

Frankie sips a thermal cup
Johnny turns a sound-bar up

Frankie learns Talmud from what the rabbis wrote
Johnny with his palm up swears another oath

While Frankie starts to rave
Johnny walks much faster

While Frankie frees a slave
Johnny offs his master

While Frankie dons a crown
Johnny tears one down

While Frankie irons his shirt
Johnny dozes in the dirt

While Frankie files reports
Johnny rinses out his shorts

While Frankie plays the hall
Johnny starts to stall

While Frankie hoes what he reaps
Johnny always plays for keeps

While Frankie inhales a bowlful
Johnny grows more soulful

Frankie falls asleep
Johnny's in too deep

Frankie sees a doctor to get his pressure read
Johnny turns the corner with a black cat bone instead

Frankie courts bewilderment
Johnny knows just what was meant

Frankie polls his consciousness
Johnny answers less & less

Frankie sees the moments form
Johnny's firmament is torn

Frankie loves to shout
Johnny's all wore out

Frankie's come too far
Johnny's where you are

Frankie worries he's been cursed
Johnny hollers "Do your worst!"

Frankie refactors the future
Johnny cooks up his past

Frankie ignores any rupture
Johnny bolts his repast

Frankie is a rose
Johnny's made of plaster

Frankie hearts what grows
Johnny is a bastard

Frankie evades disaster
Johnny courts all woes

Frankie picks his Stratocaster
Johnny clicks his toes

Frankie holes up at home
Johnny takes to the road

Frankie authors a tome
Johnny shoulders a load

Frankie & Johnny get in the car
Frankie & Johnny go too far

Frankie & Johnny won't wait for tomorrow
Frankie & Johnny waste no time on sorrow

Frankie & Johnny stare at the moon
Frankie & Johnny watch a cartoon

Frankie & Johnny under the Sun
Frankie & Johnny under the gun

Frankie & Johnny start in a minute
Frankie & Johnny see nothing in it

Frankie & Johnny sit out most games
Frankie & Johnny take one another's names

Frankie & Johnny really don't care
Frankie & Johnny tear out their hair

Frankie & Johnny feel just terrific
Frankie & Johnny read hieroglyphics

Frankie croons an all-new note
Johnny pens, "That's all she wrote"

Frankie rhymes upon his soul
Johnny abhors every goal

Frankie sings a hymn at night
To unbend the burdened soul

Johnny groans "Lend me a dime you fool.
It's time I paid my toll."

Property of the State

The harder the question the longer you wait
For an answer that puts you in an altered state
You start out strong but falter late
Your voice first sweet begins to grate
(For the tenderest tone in time must prate)
As the voice of order & the forces of fate
Speak of joy & sorrow you shift your weight
Your eyes losing focus, a response to gestate
You pray tomorrow may obliterate
Whatever the instant fails to abate
Your back turns on praise, you'd rather berate
You want to blow the lid off of this crate
Though you start out to hurry, in time fate
To erase your schedule, to blank your slate
 Rips tomorrow's halter, breaches its gate
So that once interrupted you may learn to wait
For past & future on a single date
On the day we crush the arrogant state

Away from the Garden

We come to a garden of roses
Where dew-streams drip from the thorn
While the voice of love discloses
What opens to close must mourn.

> *She tells me to walk, she tells me to talk*
> > *She is with me when I am alone*
> *What we have known we cannot share*
> > *For sparrow may not tarry with hawk.*

My love speaks; if her voice is ringing
All sound must stop & I hear
Her mute heart's violent singing
Its melody dies in air.

> *She tells me to walk, she tells me to talk*
> > *She is with me though I am alone*
> *What we have known we cannot share*
> > *For sparrow may not tarry with hawk.*

With my love in arm through a thicket
I must thread the garden paths
While in woeful voice & wicked
The garden threatens collapse.

She tells me to walk, she tells me to talk
She is with me then I am alone
What we have known we cannot share
For sparrow may not tarry with hawk.

I carry my love through a garden
In darkness around us close
When my heart begins to harden
& rose-dew menaces rose.

She tells me to walk, she tells me to talk
She is with me until I'm alone
What we have known we cannot share
For sparrow may not tarry with hawk.

Alone & Forsaken

Alone & forsaken
      that's how he was found

Wrapped in the token
      which all men once wound

In pain & quaking
      having fled the world 'round

His young heart broken
      he lay on the ground

Afraid to be taken
      by the same devil hound

Who'd silenced his joking
      to deflect his rebounds

His head he was stroking
      (it had started to pound)

While the demon raked him
      "You're a fool & a clown!

You act like you're croaking
      on some burial mound

Like you fell in a lake &
      were thoroughly drowned."

His gambit not taken
      the devil doubled down:

"Stop your drinking, dope-toking
      those nights on the town

All that snorting & smoking
      only deepens your frown.

Two eggs & some bacon
      will bring you around.

You see fakes sip on cake in
      fedoras & gowns

While the words you have spoken
      you fear to throw down.

Time to cast off your cloak &
      put on your crown!"

Users Guide to Drastic Tools

I see you there. Won't you tell me what you want.
Do you seek quality or quandary?

> Put in reverse
> it only gets worse.
> The moment it's over
> time to rehearse.

Enunciate explicitly; don't mumble in fear.
Is it a warranty? Or quarantine?

> You kiss my cheek
> better make it fast
> I might die next week
> though I plan to last.

Spit it out. Give your mission a name.
Did you say quantity? Equanimity?

> It's my property
> to triangulate fate.
> In poverty
> I'm a ward of the state.

You're back again: now what can it be?
Equality or my enmity?

> Don't pick my lock
> I may feel free.
> Don't set my clock
> Stop haunting me.

Sailor's Knot

The last of the immortals
chortles softly floating by

     BECAUSE HE KNOWS THE SUN

Touches her wreath (it's myrtle
it makes her fertile) & sighs

     WILL NEVER RISE IN HELL

She doesn't hurtle she glides
through the invisible portal

     WHEN ELSEWHERE MORNING
   COMES

to her bolthole in the sky.

     THE DEVIL RINGS HIS BELL.

Death's Dream

in memory of Hank Williams

I remember the night you first flagged me down
You asked me to give you a ride into town
God poured the moonlight into your eyes
Then in your mouth he put all those lies

When leaves filled the trees I was all your delight
When the leaves began falling, you drifted from sight
Our love was a story you read to yourself
Its pages closed, you put it back on the shelf

How my soul burned yours to discover
But you told me to turn my face to another
& our love died, a forgotten dream
Drowned beneath time's vanishing stream

On the day you left without saying goodbye
The grass at my door turned as black as the sky
Now as I wander down life's lonely way
I wonder, I ponder, why you chose to stray

Each time I feel Winter's wind unfold
I ask if, forsaken, you lie in the cold
Or alone at a window with frost on the pane
You long to be held in my arms once again

As the moments tumble into death's daily whirl
Do you ask yourself whether I'm still in this world
Will you choose one day to make a phone dial twirl
Spend another man's dime to tell me you're my girl

When the last day comes, & I fall to the ground
Your voice I will hear; it will be my last sound

   ...my stone will read:

You who walk where I lay in the sand
Know that in death's dream I still hold her hand

Lightning Strike the Right Thing

When the sun lights up the boxcar

      out back where old roads wind

In your pegged pants you parade where

      girls eye you from behind

You stroll by in your trousers

      they look you up & down

Then hooked by your superpowers

      one follows you to town

Should the Sun come up tomorrow

      leave yesterday behind

Say goodbye to pain & sorrow

      cultivate your Buddha mind

Psalms

My enemy camps on my shoulders
Rendering me disconsolate

I cannot shake the burden of his weight
Nor shift the route he takes me on

I call out Your name, but You are hidden
When I complain of his tyranny

I find my complaints never cease
But in the free moments he grants me

I repeat my every mistake
I put the whip in my enemy's hands

Like a jewel of great value
We hide in some secret place

Schooling ourselves to forget
Its location that our enemy

Cannot force us to reveal it
Time we possess soon is lost

Where our children may stumble
Upon the moment our secret

Makes it possible to recall
What now we force ourselves

To forget – that they must live
Where time at first hidden will

Unveil within Your stars.
Certain in their possession

Of its future, they will wake
To the luminance of time.

We must be patient until the moment
We hear Your voice.

But patience is unavailable to us.
It belongs only to You.

In the harmony Your voice composes
My enemy may flee

As a beast may feel ashamed
To behave in such

A human way.

Like a house with a perfect plan
Show me the limitless space You span
Like a house on its well-chosen site
Let me build my dwelling in Your light
As when he hears the bride's voice lift
The bridegroom brings the promised gift
May the arrow of my soul's intention
Pierce the membrane of Your mercy
May the songs of my soul's invention
Reach Your presence, be found worthy.

Inner Circle Out of Doors

Toward an unauthorized autobiography

Fandom Lover

While those who watch me undress

Test my trance, before too long

Here comes hazard to rip my thong

Blizzarded, O wizardess

I'm impressed; your wager won

It is you to whom I belong

Your strength will enhance my song

As you scissor me through the throng

Remedial Memorabilia I

I spent one summer long ago
        in a yurt I found abandoned
                Deep in the woods of New York State.

A guy who was camped in a lean-
        to nearby came over of an
                evening to share the gravy

& talk. Words leaped between us like
        the sparks that jump from a fire. I
                remember the odd remark he

made as I began to tire (we'd
        spent many hours talking about
                desire): "A stiff dick has taken

me places naked at midnight
        I'd fear to go in clothes by day
                with pistols at my waist." I claimed

to understand, "though I don't own
        a gun," then changed the subject: "We'll
                need some sharp forks to dent this stew."

Paying me no mind he pressed ahead:
        "Have you read what Coleridge on
                his deathbed said? 'My mind is so

clear, I might even be witty.'
        A moment later he was dead."
                When at last he had departed

I turned the coals & slept till dawn
        birds woke me & the girl I loved
                no more stopped by with news of all

I'd done or not that helped to seal
        her verdict. A few days later
                my campsite neighbor departed

& with the end of summer I
        did as well. That girl & her new
                lover my best friend followed me

way out west to the place where I
        moved next, yet her view of me would
                never yield nor alter at all.

The yurt must lie in ruins now
        or else perhaps it sports a new
                Great Room with cathedral ceiling.

That's the way things went back then, &
        they still do now. In all the woods
                where I've bedded down for one night

or for years, it's always been the
        same: no matter where I lay my
                head things keep changing all the time.

Testament in Privacy

Recounted as a dream this morning
sipping coffee by her side
the rest I don't recall.

On a telephone pole near the nest
an osprey sits this morning
to guard the nestlings.

Tiny structures piled together
at the horizon loom enormous
in a dream this morning.

About to give the nestlings their names
when a scent turns his head
the osprey sings:

> *My mate is near*
> *will soon be here.*
>
> *She bears fresh blood*
> *in her talons*
>
> *flesh for the family*
> *to share.*

These Dice Are Loaded

Chance gave me a diamond ring
                She traded it for my soul
Then seeing me neglect the thing
                She turned it back to coal

:|:

A whiskey as the sun goes down
                The long-awaited package
One more that it rise again
                Lay unopened at the door

:|:

Chance & the Moment, arm in arm
                Arrive together
                Ready to depart

They dance in one another's arms
                Chance & the Moment
                Cast off their charms

:|:

Thanks for the bag of sand you gave me
                it really does weigh a lot

Yet a single grain in my eye may feel
                    more like a stone in my shoe

Than some Sisyphean rock so heavy
                all I can do is leave it alone

:|:

               We hit the highway to the
Lost & Found, where the clerk insists
           She will never forget

(Not even when tortured or drowned
              Her final moment arrives)
The immense debt she owes our ideal,

              A gratitude that seems to grow
When it is pointed out that she
              Has neglected the matter till now.

:|:

A mockingbird's stunning routine
                    announces the punishing night
Heart bend apart this tune
                    sung in part to Mother

Put words aside & leave behind
                    this moment for another
Chance *will revise tomorrow.*

:|:

How right you are Menander
                    to ponder time at leisure
No casual other may judge
                    what you point to on your own:

Chance & the Moment
                    costumed as cousins
Hand out lessons with a laugh
                    to all who pass—
To friend & stranger alike.

Dear Tomorrow

The letters you sent
They paid my rent.
That's how far they went.
What? Did you think
They'd make us friends?
AaStEmBlUr / HloVeWeR
Now it's time to send
My afterlife stipend,
Cash for me to spend
Once I'm round the bend.

The Given Observer

Strolling in study, the given
observer wonders what time
held back may teach, mental

gestures sufficient for chance
to sew the known. Four young
guys in a Honda fetch him from

the Karachi airport at midnight.
Everywhere he directs his gaze
crowds move on roads whose

heat & darkness are bathed in red
chiaroscuro light. The forms
that reach his travel-weary eye seem

at once momentary, momentous.
A family hurtles by on a motorbike,
parents & two kids, a small

dog in the arms of one, as if
propelled by the ceaseless
din of urgencies around them.

Fists tight on the handlebars
Father fixes his eyes on their route
        for only action trimmed of

intention's wandering frame engages
        chaos, while in a silence
afforded her mind by the motorbike's

        familiar clamor Mother gazes
into a tumult of cars bikes & buses
        crossing their course repeatedly

to threaten collisions only happen-
        stance will elides while in
the Honda, eyes losing focus

        then closing, the given observer
dreams of dice that roll all lives
        back up the path to chance.

Inner Circle Out of Doors

I can't say much about
the place he chose to be

buried seven decades
or more ago. I don't

recall the location, only
that his remains lie

concealed among others
& that the six sides

of a stone memorial
star seem each to incline

toward, even gesture
at the separate paths

that once led through
undergrowth of which

no vestige remains nor
remnant of a place

where any might have
led. A visitor will find

it difficult to make out
the stone's inscription.

Is that mark a word
or a remnant of

some random incision?
But what visitor? I am

one today, in memory
& in words that also

recall, as for the
moment you are too.

Often, as a child it was
a story that led me

here, but such stories
these days are retold

infrequently. No one
is left who knows them

& few are left to hear.
Yet, location unknown,

a place may be fixed
as one's own; so it is

that these days any
path I cross seems

to offer a glimpse or
image of the marker

its chiseled message
time's wear, nothing

for time to erase. So
overgrown is the

memorial now that
I may not notice for

a while (or at all)
where I am. Of some

visits I only learn
in retrospect, if the

stone or its shadow
appear in a memory

or vice versa. Others
I may not be meant

to recall, & rarely
do, that time, but

not always, accords
a mark we call real.

I Drop a Penny in the Cup of Love

You heal the weak; you check the strong
& every time you part the throng

To right what elsewise might go wrong
(Or not) I nod, I go along

My left leg retreats as your right hand advances
I tumble into romantic trances

Calling you sister though you're xenogene
(One who summoned from a place unseen

Joins two paths as in a dream)
& never cease to echo your theme

The instant seemed that fecund
I caught your eye, I beckoned

I who thought to be no more than one
Found you instead to dote upon

Remedial Memorabilia II

As I drive the mountainous spine
Of three states today on my way
          To an annual retreat of friends

Memory's savoir faire sends me
The set Dexter Gordon played a
          Half century ago in my college

Dorm, backed by a local quartet
With Ira Sullivan on trumpet (that
          Dejected idol of Crow-Jim

Abstraction I'd so often heard Monday
Nights at the Gate of Horn's weekly
          Jam session, where he seemed to cut

Everyone who came through town)
& the pianist Jodie Christian. As
          Dexter swapped quips with listeners

Bassist Donald Garrett in his
À la Eckstine a capella way off-
          Tune baritone began to croon:

"Imagination is silly
You go around willy-nilly
             For example I go around ..."

... The car in front of me, crossing
The line after many feints, while
             I ponder memory's tonal

Scale, the way time's shutter beckons
Thought away from the wheel to where
             Revealed or else reveiled each part

Of recollection folds through the
Shadowed rectangle of a truck I pass
             To maintain speed. Forested hills

Flank the road. Sunlight flashes in
Picture windows while thin as the
             Devil's cigarillo Dexter

Tears "Cherokee" to a storm of fragments
& legendary Chicago drummer
             Wilbur Campbell turns each moment

Into music he cradles then returns.
Enormous suburban houses unroll
        Along the road like CAD drawings

    Of mausoleums with driveways.
The other tunes Dexter played I
        Don't recall. Bop classics, ballads,

    Some blues, I imagine. Yet riffs
From tenor solos roll through memory
        As if to fill out an experience

    That doesn't need the help. & now
(A different now I mean, as I write
        These lines) it's "Back Home Again

    In Indiana" that I find myself
Humming, a tune Dexter might have
        Called that day, confident it would

    Be in every player's repertoire.
So it is that each thing one knows
        May lead to another yet leave us

Suspended in motion. Time, like
This simple drive, route & endpoint known, seems
Endless! Will I get there today

I wonder, as out of nowhere
Another moment comes to mind, & I
Hear my exiled Angolan friend

Carlos recruit me to kill the
Enemy of his cause. "You fly to Rome,
Someone puts a gun in your hand.

In that moment *disparaîtra*
Ce futur que you fear eludes or
Excludes you," he goes on excitedly

While I think, Is he nuts? & fake
A chuckle as if we both know
He's joking. Heady times. Or so

They seemed, that these days gather dust
On one of memory's neglected shelves,
Unlike the vivid afternoon

I spent cross-legged on the floor
While Dexter played, I muse. & then
        As if to lift the aegis of

Memory from this unending
Day, rush hour suddenly arrives!
        I hit my brakes & watch the sun

Descend into the stalled traffic
Around me. My back is stiff from
        Hours at the wheel. This drive is

Taking forever. It's time to rest,
I think, & pull off the road. I'll
        Make it there tomorrow, but now

Dusk gathers outside the window
Of this motel room as I write
        These lines from out of my past.

Wait for Him

My eyes are small
     chin fallen &

Weighing features
     that way would you

Not find me lack-
     ing virtue too?

Death idles his
     car at the curb

To finish what
     he's reading &

I read too while
     I wait for him.

Postface: *Poetry & Chance*

1.

I moved away from San Francisco in 1992 but returned often in the years that followed to visit my daughter Sarah and see old friends, mostly poets. On one such trip West in the mid-1990s, Jackson Mac Low and I met for lunch at the Zuni Café on Market Street.

I parked around the corner, on Gough Street, and cut through a narrow alley to reach the café. Turning onto Market I spied Jackson, who had just arrived; he was taking a seat at the last in a line of outside tables that descended from Zuni's front door.

I joined him. It was an early spring day, warm and cloudless. We sat under a sky whose blue retained a cool California winter hue despite the pleasant air around us.

I knew Jackson fairly well by then, but as a fellow poet, as a comrade more than as a friend. That day, however, something got us talking in a personal way, and we soon learned that both of us hailed from Chicago. This was a pleasing coincidence.

A moment later, we discovered that we also shared a birthday. Jackson was born in 1922, on September 12. Exactly twenty years later, on the same date in 1942, I was born. Another oddity.

"Where were you born; what hospital?" I asked him. "St. Luke's Presbyterian," he replied. "That's where I was born!"

Then,
Jackson: *Where did you go to college?* Tom: "The University of Chicago. How about you?"
Jackson: "I went there too."

How strange & delightful these coincidences, these commonalities, seemed. As it turned out, we had also studied with a few of the same professors, most notably the philosopher Richard McKeon, whose classes we'd both taken as undergraduates, and David Grene, a classicist with whom I'd worked as a graduate student on the Committee on Social Thought & who had been a young faculty member in the Classics Department when Jackson studied with him.

There followed a few moments of silence. My book *Prospect of Release* had just appeared, & I'd brought a copy for Jackson. He opened it & began reading to himself. The book is a sonnet sequence that treats of a pair of doppelgangers, my biological father Thaddeus Poeller, who died when I was four, and Paul Mandel, who married my mother & adopted me, thus becoming my second father.

When our conversation resumed a few moments later, it had changed character. We too were a pair of doppelgängers, & our talk turned intimate.

Jackson read one of the poems aloud. Then he reread a few of the lines, intoning them with an emphatic eloquence.

Prospect of Release makes use of materials from Jewish theology and ritual related to fatherhood, death, & mourning. Looking up from the book, Jackson said, "I'm Jewish too."

"I had no idea," I responded, "but I'm not surprised."

"I was when I found out," he replied.

I realized, suddenly, that I should have been surprised by this news, very much surprised: earlier in our conversation, Jackson had mentioned growing up in Kenilworth, a North Shore suburb of Chicago with which I was familiar. Anyone who bought a home in Kenilworth was required to sign a contract binding him not to sell his house to a Jew. Called covenants, contracts of this kind were common at the time.

Just then, a waiter arrived bearing the platter of fried calamari we'd ordered to share. As we enjoyed our dish of *trayf,* I mentioned what I knew of Kenilworth and queried him further:

"What do you mean, when you 'found out?' When? How?"

Jackson took a swallow of wine before answering. "I was about 12. Alone in the house one day, I busied myself rummaging through the drawers of my Father's desk & came upon some old papers in a folder – immigration papers for a 'Michelovsky' family. This was our family, obviously. On the first page was a notation identifying us as Jews.

"'Mac Low' must derive from 'Michelovsky,'" he continued. "Somehow, I don't remember how, I got the idea that my mother's family was Jewish too."

"Did you ever bring this up with your parents?" I asked. Jackson replied that he'd seen no point in discussing it with them.

I told Jackson some of my own family history. After a while, with I think a mutual sense of relief, our conversation moved on to other subjects, & we gabbed in a relaxed & lively way about books & friends.

Leaving the Zuni, Jackson & I walked together up Market Street. After a minute or so, I stopped. "I'm the other way," I said. We made our goodbyes & parted.

2.

In the days that followed, my thoughts returned to our conversation. There must be a resonance, it seemed to me, between Jackson's startling discovery & the place of chance in his poetic project.

Yet, concerning a factor as pervasive as chance, any thesis one might formulate would be reductive. Chance shapes all lives, and doubtless all art too, more powerfully than intention or choice.

I found myself thinking as well about Jackson's son, Mordecai, whom I had met a few times in the late 1980s when he lived in San Francisco. "Mordecai" is a biblical name. In the Scroll of Esther, he is her older cousin & guardian; he helps her foil a plot to kill all the Jews of the Babylonian Empire.

Yet, "Mordecai" is by no means a Jewish name: it means "creature of Marduk," the great Mesopotamian god and patron deity of Babylon. For that matter, "Esther" is simply the Babylonian goddess "Ishtar," written in Hebrew letters.

In short, these are names of hidden Jews. They are the first in the written record, but there have been many more since those distant days, including Jackson Mac Low. Had his son's name been chosen to memorialize

– to hint at – his own hidden history, I wondered? What role had Iris Lezak, Mordecai's mother, played in choosing the name?

3.

I never got to ask these questions. A few days after our lunch I flew back to the East Coast. Although Jackson & I were in each other's company a number of times in the years that followed, an occasion did not arise for us to spend time alone together.

To whom else, I often wonder, did Jackson tell this remarkable story from his past? Can I be the only one who knows that Jackson Mac Low was a Jew? It seems impossible. Yet, I can find no reference to the fact, nor to the story he told me, in any discussion of his work, not even of the early work, "7.1.11.1.11.9.3!11.6.7!4., a biblical poem."

Oddest, perhaps, is the fact that we owe this knowledge, as we owe so much else, to chance. And it is to chance as well that I owe my delight in our numerous commonalities of biography.

Jackson Mac Low died on December 8, 2004 (*may his name be for a blessing among the righteous*). I've marked the date on my calendar for 2024; perhaps chance will continue to hold our pattern true.

About Tom Mandel

Tom Mandel was born and grew up in Chicago.
He was educated in the city's jazz and blues clubs
and at the University of Chicago. He has lived in
New York, Paris, San Francisco and Washington DC.
He lives in Lewes, Delaware. He is the author
of *Realism, Letters of the Law, To the Cognoscenti, Erat,
Some Appearances, Central Europe, Ready to Go,* and
other books of poetry, as well as co-author of
The Grand Piano. His work has been anthologized in
*Post-Modern American Poetry: A Norton Anthology, In
the American Tree, 49+1: Poètes Americain.* as well as
multiple volumes of *Best American Poetry.*

About Chax

Founded in 1984 in Tucson, Arizona, Chax has published more than 240 books in a variety of formats, including hand printed letterpress books and chapbooks, hybrid chapbooks, book arts editions, and trade paperback editions such as the book you are holding. From August 2014 until July 2018 Chax Press resided in Houston-Victoria Center for the Arts. Chax is a nonprofit 501(c) (3) organization which depends on suppport from various government & private funders, and, primarily, from individual donors and readers. In July 2018 Chax Press returned to Tucson.

Our current address is 1517 North Wilmot Road no. 264, Tucson, Arizona 85712-4410. You can email us at *chaxpress@chax.org*.

Your support of our projects as a reader, and as a benefactor, is much appreciated.

You may find CHAX at https://chax.org

Text: Albertina MT Pro
Display: Gill Sans

Book Design: Charles Alexander

Printer & Binder: KC Book Manufacturing

THE HOUSE OF THE INTERPRETER

Lisa Kelly has single-sided deafness. She is also half Danish. Her debut, *A Map Towards Fluency* (Carcanet 2019), was shortlisted for for the Michael Murphy Memorial Poetry Prize 2021. She is co-Chair of *Magma Poetry* and a regular host of poetry evenings at the Torriano Meeting House, London. She has been studying British Sign Language (BSL) for several years and has a Signature Level 6 qualification in BSL. Her poems have been selected for anthologies, including *Stairs and Whispers: D/deaf and Disabled Poets Write Back* (Nine Arches Press) and the *Forward Book of Poetry*. In 2021, she co-edited *What Meets the Eye*, an anthology of poetry and short fiction by UK Deaf, deaf and Hard of Hearing writers for Arachne Press. She teaches poetry and performance, and is a freelance technology journalist. To escape noise, she walks and looks out for, among other things, fungi.

THE HOUSE
OF THE
INTERPRETER
LISA
KELLY

CARCANET POETRY

First published in Great Britain in 2023 by
Carcanet
Alliance House, 30 Cross Street
Manchester, M2 7AQ
www.carcanet.co.uk

A CIP catalogue record for this book is
available from the British Library.

ISBN 978 1 80017 312 5

Cover image © Nina Thomas
Book design by Andrew Latimer
Printed in Great Britain by SRP Ltd, Exeter, Devon

MIX
Paper from
responsible sources
FSC   FSC® C014540
www.fsc.org

The publisher acknowledges financial
assistance from Arts Council England.

Supported using public funding by
ARTS COUNCIL
ENGLAND

CONTENTS

I. CHAMBER

II. OVAL WINDOW

III. CANAL

I. CHAMBER

SIGN LANGUAGE OF HOME

Fingers are not fluent in this tips-to-tips roof as if hands in prayer
have been prised apart leaving finger-pads to take fingerprints –
a tentative tent, but this temporary refuge is signed by a sharp-angled
collapse, allowing unfamiliar air and absence to intervene.

What of my Danish *hjem*, not at home on my tongue or in my hands?
A basic beginning in *tegnsprog* makes my right hand dive for shelter
under the welcoming curve of my left, fingers finding freedom,
venturing for air, only when they feel the warmth of flesh.

Is this what it is like for us all? Always having to relearn home
with a strange tongue and alien hands, prepared to open our mouths
as if to beg, to touch tongue-tip with fingertip to reveal ourselves?
This *tunge* signs almost the same in my native sign.

This tongue sounds almost the same in my estranged mother *tunge*,
if it does not fall on my deaf ear, if we can look to a gesture of home.

THE HOUSE OF THE INTERPRETER

1.

In the House of the Interpreter, the telephone is king.
In the House of the Interpreter, the telephone can ring
at any time.

Hello, this is your Audiologist.
Hello, this is your Ear, Nose and Throat Specialist.
Hello, this is God with his wishlist.

In the House of the Interpreter, there is an ur-telephone,
an early telephone, made by an 'experimenter'.
I thought of that word,
the different materials experimenters experiment with
and the different people experimenters experiment on.

Er, sorry, the receiver is on my deaf ear.
Er, sorry, I do not want an operation, but I know as my consultant,
you are not going to consult me. I am seven years old.
Er, sorry, I have nothing to confess that you would wish to hear.

2.

In the House of the Interpreter,
the ur-telephone is made of materials:
copper (alloy), metal (unknown) and wood (unidentified).

In the House of the Interpreter,
calls are unanswered and connections are missed.
Allies are unknown and unidentified.

3.

In the House of the Interpreter, there is a stained-glass window
above a pair of Bell telephones, and scratched on the stone lintel:

'Saint John of Beverley
Patron Saint of Deaf people'

You hold a model of a monastery
with your left hand.
With your right hand
you hold a crosier
decorated with a gold fleur de lis
and a flower-shaped ruby.
Your eyes are shut in saintly reverie.
Saint John of Beverley,
how do you sign?
How do you see?

4.

In the House of the Interpreter,
consonants are lost and dropped letters litter the floor.

In the House of the Interpreter,
in the hinged wooden case
for the pair of Bell telephones,
underneath the label 'WITH CARE'
I found a yellowed newspaper cutting:

MILAN CONFERENCE,
ALEXANDER GRAHAM BELL
ARGUES FOR A COMPLETE
BAN ON SIGN LANGUAGE

5.

In the House of the Interpreter,
S. M. James copied you
with copper, metal, wood and screws,
with air and density,
with electricity and intensity,
S. M. James copied you.

In the House of the Interpreter,
Theresa Dudley copied you
with an ivory plug and a feather she blew,
with lips blown apart to sound 'P' *most satisfactorily,*
with two-hour sessions of Visible Speech therapy,
Theresa Dudley copied you.

6.

In the House of the Interpreter, Abbé Serafino Balestra
left a voice message recorded on an answer machine:

Hello, this is your theologist.
The minister of Christ must open
the mouth of the deaf.
The mutes must speak.

It was easy to delete. I pressed a button.

7.

In the House of the Interpreter,
Oralism and Manualism, like Passion and Patience,
are rewarded differently and at different times.

Hello, this is your Interpreter. What is your wishlist?

EAR TRUMPET, POSSIBLY USED DURING A PERIOD OF MOURNING, EUROPE, 1850–1910
(Science Museum Group Collection)

1.

In life she listened to me. Or at least tried.
Out of kindness, I raised my voice
to make her understand. Now I have died,
my dumb widow must mourn. My choice
of ear trumpet will be held to her deaf ear
with its ornate black lace collar and bow.
I warned on my death bed, Nothing to fear
if you occupy your hand with this gift I bestow.
She paled when I raised the spectre of the Workhouse,
reminded the sweet simpleton of the Institute for the Deaf.
Speech is a divine spark. My mute grey mouse
must listen for the ghost of her better half.

2.

Today, I stand naked as a sylph dressed in air.
He is under the ground and I float above his grave.
I frolic in front of a glass with the trumpet to my ear.
Its black lace bow looks dandy – this I will save,
rip it from its hard shaft and pin it to my curls.
The black lace collar will be food for the moths.
Look now at this denuded amplifying cone, its bare shell.
Let me fill it with cream to spill on mourning cloth,
or plant it in the heap of fresh earth that covers his bones,
cut a single white trumpet flower to place in its O.
It will bind him to his voice, as the north wind groans.
My hands are free to sign in their natural flow.

RESEARCHES IN ELECTRIC TELEPHONY – A COUPLING

On 31st October 1877, Professor Alexander Graham Bell delivered a lecture before The Society of Telegraph Engineers.

It is well known that deaf mutes are dumb
well known such terms must be undone

merely because they are deaf
clearly offensive to the Deaf

and that there is no defect in their vocal organs
and they reject oral programmes

to incapacitate them from utterance
that propagate they have no voice.

Hence it was thought that my father's system
in hindsight we think your father's system

of pictorial symbols
dictatorial symbols

popularly known as visible speech
notoriously known as visible speech

might prove a means whereby we could teach the deaf
instead, the Deaf could teach us Sign Language

and dumb to use their vocal organs and to speak
for Sign Language is a visual language.

The great success of these experiments
the unforeseen success of any experiments

urged upon me the advisability of devising
means revising what is visible, risible –

methods of exhibiting the vibrations of sound optically,
how we see the reverberations of sound

for use in teaching the deaf and
taught how the Deaf fought against

dumb.
oralism.

BLACKBIRD AND BEETHOVEN

Blackbird, you are *the Beethoven of songbirds*
but when I hear this, the metaphor summons
his bust and I can't recall your call.

How many musicians, blackbird, are deaf
like the percussionist who taught herself to hear
with parts of her body other than her ears,

who performs barefoot to feel the music better?
If I'd known more about vibrations, blackbird,
how we hear with our hands with special nerve cells,

known that hearing, blackbird, is an audio-tactile experience,
with both senses tuned to environmental oscillations,
I could have countered his anecdote, the conductor

who claimed the percussionist was fake because she looked
round when he entered her dressing room. Blackbird, I
would have sung out your *chink chink* warning call.

When I see you in the ivy, blackbird,
I think of the thirteen ways of looking at you
and how you are a sign as well as a song.

Blackbird, you came before and after Beethoven,
your shaped phrases and motifs recorded
in his pocket notebook. You sing the opening

to the rondo of his violin concerto. I see him, blackbird,
as his housekeeper saw him – pencil in mouth,
a yellow beak, touching the other end to the soundboard

of a piano to feel the vibration of your song. Blackbird,
as he hits the notes harder, as the piano starts
to fall apart, will the fake musicians turn round?

Today, I am not so deaf.
The wind is undeafening me, I think.
The window is to my right ear, my hearing ear.

I can hear the wind, alright, oh yes, it is raucous,
but the cool draught on my right cheek
coming through the rickety frame, is gentle.

Yesterday evening, I went to Deaf Club.
I met with two of the group beforehand.
We are friends through BSL class. They are not deaf.

One is in love with a guy who is not deaf,
but is a BSL interpreter – his parents are deaf.
On the way home, she says that deaf people are too direct.

'They ask direct questions. They make me feel awkward.'
She has been working in a Deaf Café, and gives an example
of how a deaf person asks for coffee in BSL:

Coffee (forefinger and thumb of dominant hand make a C shape,
*   tipped by the mouth)*
Now (hands come down hard in front of the body, palms flat and
*   face up)*

'That's just Deaf culture. That's just how BSL works,' she says.

I wonder if I am too direct.
I think I am direct but am unsure
if this is my nature or my deafness.
If you have to look people straight in the face,

if you have to keep eye contact, watch lips and focus,
it is direct behaviour.

I think of animals like dogs,
how a stare is considered a threat.
How you are advised to look away or look down.

What are you looking at? barks the man in the bar,
and you look away or look down.
Perhaps being indirect is the safest option.

The other friend is a dancer.
She is expressive.
I like watching her sign.
She is unsure of the guy who sat next to her.
His sign name is Fox – right hand around his nose
drawing out into a pointy snout.

>

I couldn't pick up his English name,
he fingerspelt too fast. Miles, I think.
(*the quick brown fox…*)

She is trying to work out whether he is coming onto her,
or whether he is just too direct and she is
misinterpreting his directness for attraction.

I think back to the number of men
who have misinterpreted my concentration
on what they were saying as attraction.

My direct stare —
a direct invitation of sorts
for a kiss.

The wind is not settling down. I doze off:
The dogs have dissected my soul
and what is lost suggests itself in absence.

Dream thoughts are wild and senseless,
yet have a pleasing music. I translate
quickly, or I forget, and the page is silent.

FROM D/dIARIES: *TUESDAY AFTERNOON, THINKING OF GETTING A HAIRCUT, 12TH FEBRUARY 2019*

I remember trying to lipread
my hairdresser's small talk
looking in the mirror
while the hairdryer
blew hot air into my hearing ear
as he styled the right side
of my head.

I remember looking
at my teenage face and watching
it grow redder and redder
as I nodded and smiled
at what I hoped were the right cues.

CALL AN AIRBORNE LOVED ONE

My right fist is a handset: my thumb the earpiece,
little finger the mouthpiece. Now my fist is horizontal,

finger and thumb are the wings of a plane
coming in to land at the airport of my open left palm,

thumb wing tilted on Mount of Venus.
Do the ears of the imaginary people pop?

Have they turned on their phones? Yes or no?
Which? My horizontal fist and indicative digits shake

from side to side, the calloused airstrip falls away.
Passengers of this ham-fisted pilot suffer turbulence.

They need a restorative glass of wine – tip thumb flute
and little finger stem to lips to ferment the flow of flesh

before the back of my fist is stuck to my forehead with
hex finger and little finger horns. This is how the devil looks,

jealous of all things that fly and land safely. Think
of sound waves travelling at the speed of love. Maybe –

my fist vibrates, little finger and thumb cocked – it is time
to make that call. My right fist is a handset:

my thumb the earpiece, little finger the mouthpiece.
I think of all the calls that were never heard.

BSL TOPIC COMMENT STRUCTURE

Imagine you hold a piece of chalk
and there's a blackboard.

Go up to it, and draw a man
standing on a bridge.

Have you drawn a stick man,
his legs dangling in mid air

and quickly added the arch of the bridge
to meet his little stick feet?

Or have you, quite naturally,
first drawn the bridge, then the man

with his feet of two chalk dashes
cresting the crown?

I put down the piece of chalk
having drawn my first lesson.

MICHELANGELO, LEARNING BSL LINGUISTICS WITH FLASHCARDS ON THE TREADMILL,

is a gradient of 15 with a walking speed of 5
enough to make you puff, but not hit the red trapezoid.

Increasing the speed to 6 while trying to understand
the difference between topographic and syntactic space

is recreating a map of the real world in the signing space
above the console where the gym is opposite the park, versus –

the strength of the weightlifter in the space by the safety key
compared to the flexibility of the Yogi suspended over the
        cupholder.

Holding the handrail so as not to collapse is grasping
the concept of the handling classifier 'FIVE' which shows

how your hand morphs into a steel claw in an attempt
to unscrew the ridiculously tight lid of your protein powder.

Demonstrating the conditional by raising your eyebrows
and tilting your sweating brow slightly forward is letting your
        towel

drape over the handrail if it promises not to fall on the belt.
Recognising an iconic sign is catching a glimpse

of your agonised face in the mirror, and tracing the path
of a tear drop with your right index finger down your cheek.

Acknowledging that negation comes after a negative
as in *he died on the treadmill, no* is narrowing your eyes,

shaking your head and passing your palm across pursed lips
with the mouth pattern 'BOO' when asked for information.

Accepting that aspect is the internal timing of an event is interrupting
your session to hurriedly retie your laces. To finish jubilantly

by swigging from a water bottle and punching a fist in the air
is using movement to show meaning as universal gesture.

THE APPLE OF DISCORD

for the most in need

No gods, or goddesses, weddings, or wars.
Eris returns a flaccid bag of apples.
One at the bottom, half-eaten, a browning core.

My co-worker signs, and I interpret, 'What for?'
'The taste is rotten.' We don't want a battle.
No gods, or goddesses, weddings, or wars.

The tacit question, in Sign or English, makes us pause.
For £1.82, we're not prepared to haggle.
One at the bottom, half-eaten, a browning core.

Why eat so many before returning to the store?
With what's unsigned, unsaid, a manager can grapple.
No gods, or goddesses, weddings, or wars.

Mouths and hands move in awkward rapport.
Eris wants a refund – not a gift card's hassle.
One at the bottom, half-eaten, a browning core.

If this is a scam, we can't translate the cause.
We have customers to serve. Not tackle.
No gods, or goddesses, weddings, or wars.
One at the bottom, half-eaten, a browning core.

LUCKY DIP FOR SEDNA

Your father cut off your fingers
as you clung to the kayak,
and the freezing waters skirted your waist.

You sank to the ocean floor and your fingers
became seals, walruses, and whales.
You grew a fishtail and ruled the deep.

Now, at the counter, wearing blue gloves,
you have chosen Lucky Dip.
My finger and thumb shape an 'L'

that touches the tip of my nose
before picking something from the air
and Karolina signs Wednesday or Saturday?

And you will dive in on Saturday,
cling to the hope of fair winds,
swish a fishtail skirt if you win –

the violence of life swept away,
a cruise taking in seals, walruses, and whales.
Crossed fingers wish you good luck.

PARALLEL MOVEMENT OF THE HANDS

yes, you make sense line by line, John Ashbery,
giving, rather, the possibility of sense line by line,
but here is a customer at the front of a long line –
James Tate came up with the term 'meta-spaghetti' –
they want the price checked on a packet of spaghetti,
and my fingers are twisting out and away,
as sense twists out and away
                                    as sense twists out and away
and my fingers are twisting out and away,
they want the price checked on a packet of spaghetti,
James Tate came up with the term 'meta-spaghetti' –
but here is a customer at the front of a long line –
giving, rather, the possibility of sense line by line,
yes, you make sense line by line, John Ashbery.

ENCOUNTER

I am a centaur at the counter,
half human, half horse,
selling dog food to the man
who thinks he's human because
he chooses to use his voice.

I am a centaur at the counter,
Sagittarius my sun sign,
half hearing, half deaf,
half speech, half sign,
and I encounter this customer.

I am a centaur at the counter
carrying a quiver, am aquiver
at the words of the man,
unholy human, who says,
They are human you know.

I am a centaur at the counter,
blunt arrows in my quiver,
his Hydra-breath,
his venomous question,
Can she speak?

I am a centaur at the counter
cantering away, if I could,
from his voice, incensed –
couldn't counter, didn't censor,
bucking, harnessed.

EVERY THURSDAY LUNCHTIME,

knock-knock man makes an appearance.
He comes to cheer us up with a knock-knock joke –
the same knock-knock joke he tells every week.

Knock, knock!
Who's there?
Knock-knock man, who else?
It's Thursday lunchtime after all,
as good a time as any
for a knock-knock joke.

I want to tell him that puns don't translate into sign,
but there's a queue forming,
and two fingers tapping my torpid pulse for DOCTOR,
my right index finger circling in space for WHO?
suggests something of this Time Lord's science fiction
that he might cheer us up next Thursday lunchtime
with a knock-knock joke.

#WHEREISTHEINTERPRETER

It is always an access issue, always a case of make do,
make do with subtitles, make do with delay,
catch up because you don't matter and are relatively few.

The Prime Minister briefs on the pandemic every day,
what we should do because 'we are all in this together'
but 87,000 people cannot hear what he has to say.

In Scotland and Wales, they provide an interpreter
for vital information about how the virus is spreading,
what is expected of us, which problems might occur

if we don't understand exactly where we're heading,
if we don't stand united and follow government guidelines.
If your first language is sign, if you have no hearing

then hear this: the Deaf community should not be side-lined.
Give equal access to information for all. *We, the undersigned.*

II. OVAL WINDOW

IF MY DEAF EAR WERE A MUSHROOM

it would not be a jelly ear, only seen in winter and spring,
growing on hardwood, mainly dead elder trees –
it would be seen all year round, poking out from straggly grass;

it would not be a flea's ear, small with a dirty orange upper surface
and a tiny stem that becomes increasingly wrinkled with age –
it would grow with age and under stress, flame red;

it would not be a toad's ear, found on a forest trail
blending in with bark chippings, split down the shorter side –
it would be found on a silent path, overlooked, split between worlds;

it would not be a hare's ear, yellow with a pinkish tinge,
gathered in small groups in woods, most often with beech trees –
it would be solitary within an urban environment;

it would not be a veined ear, funnel shaped, on soil and debris,
edibility unknown and with conservation action needed –
it would be delectable and mistaken for more common species;

it would not be a moss ear, growing on living trees, facing
downwards, nestled in moss, fingernail-width and delicate –
it would face outwards, finely balanced, attuned to life's vibrations;

it would not be a silver ear, commercially cultivated for cuisine,
cures and cosmetics, tasteless but valued for its gelatinous texture –
it would be valued for signing the way to alternate reality.

How fungi communicate, thinking about the wood wide web, might
lead us to the rainforest floor beneath the understory where we
can lie, the mycelial network beneath us. Mosquito and leech will be
waiting with proboscis or sucker, attracted by our breathing, able
to sense us from five-bodies-lying-down-in-a-row away, to
suck blood to survive, lay eggs. We will bear any bites to expand
our understanding of ghost fungus, how the green glow of some
that grow from the base of a dead tree, is nothing to be afraid of.
Bioluminescence is not magic, a sprite luring us from our
path to fall into the jaws of a crocodile. Let luciferin light up concepts
of ghost fungus attracting insects in the dark to disperse spores. Such
love between species is almost magic. As misunderstood as
an alien radiance in the forest of our fears. Tonight, we are not speaking,
we are listening with our eyes. We feel for the forest as a ghost fungus might.

Hooked up to a synthesiser, the blue oyster mushrooms are not
talking, but making music through biodata sonification. John Cage always
loved mushrooms. Ate one and got sick. Wrote music that did not require
notes: *four minutes, thirty-three seconds* was not composed just for ears
but possibilities. Foraging for fungi fed music, poetry and
improvisation. *What leaf? What mushroom?* – loosely interpreting
Basho's haiku: *Matsutake; and on it the leaf of some unknown tree,* which might
be about one species' ignorance of the other, or happenstance, or not
anything we can agree on. The leaf of some unknown tree is not always
sticking to the mushroom cap. It blows off or rots. We might require
different translations. I may cook the mushroom. You may put the leaf in a
book of haiku poetry as a placeholder while other leaves flutter in a nervous
dance. Let us forage, as blue oyster mushrooms sync with the system.
What we find, how we hear is only a wonky approximation of what we are.

After Hiroshima, a mushroom was the first living thing. Events we
cannot foresee and events we can but refuse to avert, not able
to unravel threads of where one hurt begins and another ends. To
live like hyphae might be a cosmic trip: part of the mycelium, able to do
what conjures the collective, to reach out for root tips as if this
is the apotheosis of dark matter. In a teaspoon of Amazon soil, without
identification, hundreds of types of putative fungi exist without smothering
difference for pre-eminence. Hyphae blur borders, have other
ways of signalling. What mushroom cloud looms if we dismiss life
in all its 8.7 million different forms? Plastics, crude oil, explosives are forms
of waste broken down by fungi; our detritus treated like dead wood with
enzymes and adaptability. Fungi connect plants without prejudice,
swap nutrients for sugar, eat radiation like a hibiscus licks up sunshine and
co-evolve with natural or unnatural worlds. Interpretation is not innuendo.

MUSHROOM TO SVAMP

How fungi transform material, we admire
as Google, from English to Swedish,
translates mushroom into svamp.

A beautiful word, a swamp-cum-vamp,
a siren emerging from a quagmire
to appeal to our fetishistic death wish.

Alice in IKEAland swallows SVAMP,
regurgitates a lamp. We may desire
a frosted orange agaric, but our outlandish

dream is out of stock. Alice has SVAMPIG,
a grey/white sponge, the soft side, a dish-
cloth, the coarse side for stains that require

more vigorous cleaning. SVAMPIG
commands, *Wet before use*. No PISH-
SALVER, *Drink me*, but she aspires

not to shrink from tasks, nor whirl in the gyre –
materials *may be recyclable*. O Thanatos, in English
you translate. Spongy is SVAMPIG.

RED DATA LIST OF THREATENED BRITISH FUNGI: MAINLY SMUTS

Smut, lie down with me in annual meadow grass that tickles
our pelts. Smut, be barley-covered and reeking of beer,
a bearberry redleaf prim on each pinkish part. Smut, with your bedstraw hair,
bestow no interloper a bird's eye view. My promise, a primrose
with its fairy caretaker that no bog asphodel, no bone-breaker
will I brook, smut. As a chick weeds out a worm, I will weed out
all burrowing doubts, all jealousies, all winter green looks
on our love, smut, which would shrivel us, smut. Smut, be not false.
This oat-grass ring, I twine about your finger, smut.
Think of me when a foxtail, smut, lifts to expose a gland,
stinking of March violets, to deceive you, smut.
They'd have you frogbit, smut, back in the pond where you
were spawned, mounted and belly grasped. Glaucus sedge creeps
in damp ditches, smut. Weep for such green hell bore away
with earth's daughter, smut. Loose your hair. See how sedge flowers in spikelets,
smut, and love always pricks. Lie down with me in meadow grass that tickles
our pelts. Revel in mudwort, smut. I could call you close to Limosella, smut,
cloaked in tiny white stars, a northern bilberry redleaf prim on each pinkish part.
Passion marks us, smut, with a purple small-reed stripe, smut.
My rare spring sedge, smut, tender as fresh shoots.
My reed canary-grass, smut, sensitive to noxious airs. Saxifrage smut,
I cannot help but repeat saxifrage smut, the brassy instrument of you played.
Sing of prickly yuletide, sea holly smut. They are small spored
with their white beaks, sedge smut, poking and prodding and stinking, smut.
They are not sweet – they confuse carnal with vernal, smut.
Damn the white beak-sedge, smut, worn by quacks as if we were plague, smut,
with their aromatic herbs, smut. What rare pathogens we are, smut.
What gall, smut, to detest our dark teliospores. Yellow toadflax
on them all, the cowards that croak. Yellow toadflax on them all, smut.

STINKHORN

Charles Darwin's eldest daughter, Etty, destroyed all the
specimens of Stinkhorn she could find on the Darwin Estate

A warm wind blows through the wood.
Nostrils flare, sniff out adulterous odours
of phallus impudicus, its dark olive hood,

slimy with gleba for flies to feast on spores,
spread filth like lovers' carnal thoughts,
putrid, stench of carrion that angels abhor –

witch's egg, lurking to hatch but I've brought
my pointed stick, wear my hunting cloak,
good gloves, carry a basket for those caught

in flagrante delicto, blazing offence, I'll smoke
on the fire in deepest secrecy, door locked,
because of the morals of the maids, as I choke

on fumes of fornication, olfactory sense shocked
by reek of cadeverdine and putrescine,
inducing my body to spasms, feeling it rocked

by waves of revulsion at such an obscene
tang, close to the sinful stink of spermidine.

CUP FUNGI ON THE RED LIST

Consider the cups, the rare and beautiful cups,
one is a goblet, a beechwood goblet. Consider
it filling with raindrops from beech leaves, held out
by an elf, an elf with so many cups to choose from –
a mauve elfcup, a ruby elfcup, a scarlet elfcup.
Consider they are not so rare, although you may never
have seen them, and consider, whose cup runneth over?
The elf's or man's? Consider other rare cups,
golden cup and ebony cup. Consider precious metals
and trees, hammered or carved into goblets or cups,
then consider rare cups made of mycelium and how
if a golden cup bruises, its edges become blue,
and plectasin, found in ebony cup, is a rare breakthrough
in the battle against antibiotic-resistant bacteria. Consider.

MYCOLOGY ABECEDARIAN

Acrid knight, amethyst deceiver, ascot hat
bird cherry dotty, bitter poisonpie, black morel
Caesar's amanita, cinnamon jellybaby, club foot

Darwin's golfball, deathcap, destroying angel
earpick fungus, ebony woodwax, elbowpatch crust
fluted bird's nest, fly agaric, frosty funnel

glutinous earthtongue, green skinhead, ground ivy rust
hair sedge smut, horn of plenty, humpback inkcap
icicle spine, indian paint fungus, iron porecrust

Jack o lantern, jelly ear, jubilee waxcap
King Alfred's cakes/ cramp balls, king oyster
leaf parachute, loose starweb, luminous porecap

mauve elfcup, Medusa mushroom, mountain deceiver
nettle pox, northern honey fungus, nutty brittlegill
oak blackhead, ochre gillgobbler, orange bladder

pale staghorn, powdery piggyback, purple spindles
quartzy webcap, queen bolete/ bronze bolete
rainforest horsehair, rayed earthstar, redfold truffle

scarlet caterpillarclub, seablight microdot, strawberry bracket
tangerine bonnet, terracotta hedgehog, the gypsy
umbilicate hedgehog, unicorn pinkgill, upright knight

vampires bane, variable oysterling, veiled lady
weeping widow, witches' butter, woolly woodwart
'xcentric pinkgill, 'xtinct prototaxities, 'xtinction threat 400 species

yellow mascara disco, yellow stainer, yellow star-of-bethlehem smut
zeller's bolete, zoned hairy parachute, zoned rosette.

MYCELIUM

There is not one way to reproduce, to open legs,
slice belly, lay, hatch, spread seed far.
We are earthstars – Berkeley and Elegant,
Field, Flask, Rayed and Weathered, and we are rare.

We are constellations above the earth.
We listen out for rain to release what we store.
Each drop that hits a spore sac is a violence. We weep in the rain.
We dissolve and release a little more.

Powdery spores puff out from our tiny ostioles as it pours.
This immense pressure to push in every baby shower.
We split like a star, and a new universe is born.
There is not one way to unfold, to bloom or flower.

There is not one way to listen out for rain, to deliquesce,
disperse, break open, rage, decompose, sob, mourn, fray.
We are puffballs – Fen and Heath, Pedicel and Steppe.
We whisper as our spores are blown and the wind wears us away.

There is not one way to evolve, to fight for survival.
We are cannons – Bog and Dune. Hidden in mud or sand.
We are stalkballs, and a stiltball – Scaly, White, and Sandy.
Sometimes to look dead, lie low, be insignificant is pre-planned.

There is not one way to be threatened, to become extinct.
We are Dung Bird's Nest and Pepper Pot, and we are ingenious
with rain-splash cups and small holes to shake out spores.
There is more than one way to protect, to continue, to save us.

FUNGI ARE A DIFFICULT GROUP TO CREATE RED LISTS FOR

after Liz Holden

Questions about extinction are not straight forward.
We only see the fruiting structure –
filamentous cells, mostly invisible in soil and wood,
but fruit bodies are not always produced.
Are fungi rare fruiters rather than truly rare?

MUSHROOM

You are in the dark as you write. Literally in the dark –
scribbling lines on top of lines under the stairs,
in the cupboard, squashed near a broom handle.
Hope something heavy will not fall on your head
from the shelf with its bric-a-brac and useless tools.
Try not to think about it. Try to think like a mushroom.

Somewhere a scientist prescribes magic mushrooms
for their psychoactive properties to get you out of a dark
place, unravel a knotty problem. Another tool
to fix the human condition. Darkness vibrates with steps on stairs.
Silence is best for thoughts to bloom inside your head,
aspire to magical thinking, an alternative way to handle

what you must grapple with. Lately, you sought to handle
a mushroom – passed a woman holding mushrooms
like a bunch of flowers, delicately, with her head
bent over them in the rain, looking tenderly at their dark
brown caps. She had descended the concrete flight of stairs
to the patch of meadow where volunteers use tools

to cut back brambles, dig the Butterfly Border. Tools
are provided by the small charity, a not too heavy to handle
mower. The main thing is connectedness. Under the stairs,
you think about mycelium, that when you see a mushroom,
it is the fruiting body that has untangled itself from the dark
to push through, how it develops from a nodule or pinhead

near the surface of the substrate, how this two-millimetre head
burgeons into a button, breaks its universal veil, and basic tools –
fingers and thumbs – do the job of foraging in the dark

matter of rot and soil, decay that is difficult to handle.
You traced the woman's tracks to where the mushrooms
grew, and picked one. Now like hyphae, under the stairs

the universal veil is cobwebs in the spandrel of the stairs;
lines on top of lines, scribbled in spider script; your head
filled with rot and ruin, as you try to think like a mushroom,
perhaps a shelf fungus supported by a bracket like the tools
on the shelf with its missing bracket. The loose handle
to the cupboard could drop off and keep you in the dark –

no psychedelic mushroom, no mystical insight under the stairs.
The mushroom you picked is also in the dark; its soft brown head
decomposing as writing tools make mycelium. You turn the handle.

AMANITA MUSCARIA

Looking for a flash of red in the green,
I walked the path through the valley.
October, and a hint of russet gleamed,

but anthocyanin had turned a leaf ruby,
and it tricked my eye in the long grass,
an experience not exactly hallucinatory,

an illusion of sorts, if one thing can pass
for another, one sense not make sense
of what is sensed. Did this mistake class

as foreshadowing the effects – the intense
colours, mood shifts, visual distortion –
of ingesting muscimol. A cat in branches

disappears into a grin. Frabjous perception
of unseen fly agaric, berserker mushroom.

MUSHROOM STONES

The sculptures were thought to be phallic symbols only, a theory that still crops up occasionally but that must be rejected as one-sidedly male-centred
– drugtimes.org

And some believed they were idols
And some believed potter's tools
And some believed they were markers
And some believed they were stools

And some believed the cap was female
And some believed the cap should be licked
And some believed the stem was male
And some believed the stem should be kicked

And some believed in ancient cultures
And some believed in cults
And some believed in counterculture
And some believed in guilt

And some believed in mycophobes
And some believed in mycophiles
And some believed in psychedelic strobes
And some believed in a cat that smiles

ALTERNATE REALITY

Because sometimes there are bits of ourselves we just can't deal with.
Coping mechanisms are exhausted.
Dead inside sort of describes it –
everything is too much effort and we crave
feelings, aliveness, call it fecundity. The hospitalised
guy who injected himself with psilocybin,
his name withheld, could be any one of us,
imposters in the great game of surviving ups and downs,
just hanging on, and when Polly puts the
kettle on, why not make it a brew worth the risk of kidney failure,
liver failure. Surely,
magic comes with risk and boiling down shrooms into a mushroom tea, after
noting the potential therapeutic effects of hallucinogens in
online research is understandable, relatable.
Psychoactive effects from psilocybin could be a miracle cure, but the
question is, how we do things –
recreationally or destructively.
Shrooms leading to multisystem organ failure, fungus growing in your blood,
treatment in intensive care, and a prescription of long-term antifungal drugs is
ugly and unexpected despite any compensating
vivid flashbacks, or in medical terms, hallucinogenic-induced persisting deception
    disorder.
What are we going to do with reality?
Xtc, etc. is illegal, but taking the edge off with a natural high –
you have at least thought about it haven't you? The relief of reaching an alternate
zone of being.

MYCELIUM LAMPSHADE

We are looking for new materials in our material life.
Here, in this wood, goat willow grows but snaps easily.
But over there, look how two branches of a hazel tree
are bound by something that could hold us all together
to face a dim future. We want shade from the light.
It is dark in the wood, and we dare not talk of bare bulbs,
their awful glare. Please give us something softer,
something much diffused so we can coo over the bulbs
in the ground glorying in the nurturing dark. Give us
hardy and compostable, hoof fungus and wood chip,
give us something that doesn't break with the strain
of all our interior designs. We are done with the hide
stretched; we are sickened by Sylvia's skin; we abhor
the horror of the Plainfield Ghoul's anthropodermic
trophies, but we cannot hide from a myth stretched
beyond the sustainable; mycelium as mystic resource –
if what hangs in the understorey costs a week's wage
while we feast in the zero-waste restaurant on truffle oil.

DARNING MUSHROOM

humans share nearly 50% of their DNA with fungi
– Paul Stamets, mycologist

My big toe is blooming from the hole in my sock
like a mushroom. It is pale and uninspiring,
and could be a button mushroom, mass-produced,
grown on manure, and not very tasty looking.

The sock is a somewhat more glamourous substrate,
worth saving from this fruiting body and its assault
on the mesh of blue wool fibres, like a stinkhorn,
phallus impudicus, poking its way through asphalt.

In a lightbulb moment, I insert one; the sock is stretched
over to expose the hole in a bulbous O
inviting my needle to pick up a stitch at the edge
to criss-cross with hyphae-like threads, as I sew

loosely from right to left until, towards the apex,
stitches come closer, thread is gently pulled
to close the hole, finishing with a little looped knot.
Let my toe do subterranean work, like a prized truffle.

DARK HONEY FUNGUS

Last, love, if you can, for as long as Oregon,
where your forsaken honey, Armillaria Ostoyae,
is this earth's largest organism. Pray,
as I creep through soil in the Blue Mountains,
your transgressive hands – dabbling in the sin
of Armillatox so thick black tendrils cannot stray –
do not burn. Centuries-old rhizomorphs fray
brittle nails scooping the squares of miles I count in.

Lest, love, you forget my yellow-capped fruiting body,
I will glow in the dark, greenly, for you.
Bioluminescence on a moonless night glimpsed through
firs, is a figment of leaf-lit gills, a ghostly
reminder of our pathogenic liaison, an unseemly
desire to spread spores to new worlds where few
survive beyond our all-conquering ambition to
destroy every root in the name of monstrosity.

List, love, reasons our non-vegetable love failed.
Vaster than empires we grew, colonised ecosystems,
devoured forests; an endless appetite for lignum,
our shared heterotrophic sympathies unveiled
a common network of cells, but your needs prevailed.
Timber-fuelled investment and you kissed capitalism,
as I prowled ponderosa pine, white larch. Our schism
sworn on a rotten growth ring as chainsaws wailed.

Lost love, do you recall you picked my sweet flesh
blooming on bark, threw my tough stem in needle litter?
When your incisive pearls sliced through, did I taste bitter?
You forgot I must be cooked thoroughly, began to thresh

as I danced in your gut, your face a hot flush.
Had you stopped to lift the bark, you might have felt fitter –
on seeing my white web of mycelia, thought better
of consuming any part of me. Conceived how I enmesh.

Lust, love, is always longing close to home. You quail
at mycelia, the weight of a blue whale in Oregon
but look to your garden at Mellea, sticky for rhododendron,
gooseberry, flowering currant, wisteria that scales
to escape my spreading, invading, girding. Tall tales
of white latex coating plants to build my stores of glycogen.
You would starve me of water, oxygen. Our rotten
ways, but Armillaria will outlive you. A mere detail.

FOR ALL THE DIRT EATERS

The red plague rid you
        For learning me your language!
    – Caliban, *The Tempest*

For all the dirt eaters who have tasted earth,
put soil in their mouths to savour root, rot, how the leaves
fell, the fungi translated dead matter into minerals.
For all the dirt eaters who have buried their faces
in loam, craved clay, crunched chalk, inhaled deeply
for a scent of moss, worms, mustiness, petrichor.
For all the dirt eaters – my sisters, my brothers, my others –
who understand that a tap root must go to such depths,
that mycorrhizal fungal networks swap sugar for nutrients.
For all the dirt eaters who have taken they know not what
into their gut, whose gut instinct is survival, who have been forced
to spit sullied words, had their mouths moulded into shapes
they did not desire. For all the dirt eaters whose tongues
have circled stomata – for transpiration, for oxygen, for water –
sensed them open and close, whose hands have been tied to a bed frame
for opening and closing, for framing a sign. For all the dirt eaters
who have been locked in a coal bunker until their mouths are clean.
For all the dirt eaters who have lifted their hand – palm to face –
in shame, then licked along each crease – the heartline,
the headline, the lifeline, and clung on. For all the dirt eaters
who have clawed their cheeks with index and middle fingers,
who know this sign for shit is the truth of shame, who have seen it
for a sham, who have been cheated of their land, their culture,
who have been taught language, and their profit is they know how to curse.
For all the dirt eaters, who will not be styed in a hard rock,
who know the hum of twangling instruments about ears
is the hum of humanity, the hum of humus, the hum of exhumed,
ashes to ashes, dust to dust, dirt to dirt. For all the dirt eaters,
who, with their long nails, keep digging for pignuts.

SCARLETT CATERPILLAR CLUB

Who begot the gap must gawp at the gape between species crossed

What sort of society are you?
Sounds like one I'd wish to join –
vivid, kind of cute, definitely can-do
with undulating segments and all those implied legs.

I look you up for entry requirements:
Are you a fan of the great outdoors?
You might enjoy grasslands or woodlands.
Looking for a change – willing to metamorphose?

Yes, that's me, an Emperor Moth caterpillar.
I'm up for selection; to be sprinkled with special spores.
Just the lucky few, mind. We get to settle down
in sexy soil or luxurious leaflitter. Begin to pupate.

O, to be in an exclusive club. The thought of it
turns your insides to mush, causes your head to explode
with a bright orange fungus. Club motto:
Need it like a hole in the head.

ANOTHER RIDDLE

Been bitten by one and eaten the other,
had a red rash and a full belly.

One type that bit me cultivates the other
in Mexico, South and Central America,

can lift pieces of leaves, like a mother
can lift a car to save her trapped child.

Dangerous for one to forage for the other,
dodge flies laying eggs in crevices of heads.

Larvae of one can't live without the other,
feasting on its swollen hyphal tips.

Work of one means no spores of the other –
kept in the colony free from mould and pests.

Does a mutualistic relationship smother
the urge to strike out alone, to become other?

MUSHROOM MACHINE

The urge to begin with 'I'
must be resisted. This default mode
close to the manufacturer's setting
most users would probably choose.
Brain at wakeful rest, daydreaming
about which lock 'I' fits
to start the whole engine churning.

Alan Turing is on the new £50 note.
His nephew says he should be remembered,
not primarily for code-breaking, but for
asking, 'Can machines think?'
Our smartphones can write plausible poetry.
The Computer's First Christmas Card
does not begin *iwishyou*.

Professor Adamatzy inserted electrodes
in oyster mushrooms and held a flame
to the cap of one. Other fruiting bodies
responded in the mycelial network
with a sharp electrical spike –
potential for fungal computers
and mycelium as environmental sensors.

Time of year: autumn; adjective: electric;
two singular nouns, not normally
in the same sentence: mushroom, machine;
another adjective: pale; verb: signals.
Electric autumn
An oyster mushroom signals
Beyond the machine

'SIX WAYS MUSHROOMS CAN SAVE THE WORLD'
– Paul Stamets, mycologist

I'm in love with the old-growth forest.
The screen has frozen on the Ted Talk,
the static caption, a guru's gift.

I watch the spinning wheel icon,
the endless O, like a dog chasing its tail,
or a ferret in a ring, then run out of similes.

Dusty (I caught her name before stasis)
holds a green basket with a red stripe
and is looking down at the forest floor.

Maybe I'll watch the wheel spin forever,
the moss-covered trunks, the meditative Dusty
whose beautiful dark hair hangs loosely.

She looks like she is going on a picnic
in the old-growth forest, mycelium
beneath her feet feeding those huge firs.

The mycologist might be a magician who has
vanished. In one hundred years, who will wake
and say, *I'm in love with the old-growth forest.*

MYCOLOGY

Mum forwent foraging.
Only ever spoke of a childhood
on Copenhagen's clay courts –
tennis balls, never puffballs.

My eye is untrained, a novice pupil.
Dad fared better – once he
brought back silky mushrooms
ribbed with papery brown gills.

He fried them for Sunday lunch
which mum believed almost unholy,
not that she was religious,
but placing a possible poison

on the family table broke
a sacrament of sorts. That smell –
the almost-meaty mushrooms frying
in garlic and butter was tantalising.

He would have let me dig
my fork into what he swore was a
field mushroom, found where
horses manured the ground,

but mum's warning, *You could die,*
difficult to ignore. A lesson in
how pleasure can serve up mortality –
a lesson I try to teach my son.

Dad didn't die. Not then.
Now I find myself tramping fields,
head down, like Mammon
possessed by mushrooms –

focused on finding and identifying,
not picking and consuming,
but the quest is ongoing,
and one day I hope

to fry a mushroom medley
in the finest Danish butter,
and pass on my knowledge,
having eaten of the earth.

IN SEARCH OF COWBANE RUST

Daughter, Son, some rusts are rare
Their hosts are rare, that's why
If I'm long gone, don't despair
I'm on the Broads with watchful eye

Their hosts are rare, that's why
I paddle down Wheatfen dyke
I'm on the Broads with watchful eye
Slipping off with otter and pike

I paddle down Wheatfen dyke
Checking for cowbane at the edge
Slipping off with otter and pike
Fingers brushing willow and sedge

Checking for cowbane at the edge
I found clumps, but none had rust
Fingers brushing willow and sedge
Hope of a parasite come to dust

I found clumps, but none had rust
If I'm long gone, don't despair
Hope of a parasite come to dust
Daughter, Son, some rusts are rare

WATERY MILKCAP

O little baby with your sweet brown head
O little baby with your damaged gills
O little baby with our clumsy tread
O little baby with your milky spills

O little baby with your bloom so rare
O little baby with your love of oak
O little baby with our devil-may-care
O little baby with your wrinkled cloak

O little baby with your Latin name
O little baby with your Lactarius serifluus
O little baby with our mycophobic shame
O little baby with your scorn for *poisonous*

III. CANAL

WATERMARK

Filled not with champagne, but with tap water –
a cut glass coupe from Charles, the only one left,
rim cloudy with limescale from the dishwasher.
Should have washed by hand, but care is not deft.
Here on a window ledge, some strange refraction –
I can see through the water, a man who stands
in the street below; the optic trick has fascination.
Though I care for physics like washing by hand,
this bend in light direction is fine, like champagne.
Three sips to half drain the glass. Back on the ledge
more shadows, more cloud, more of the mundane.
The man has disappeared, but I would hedge
my bets he remains. A final gulp, an empty coupe –
that holds no crystal-lit water to warp life's loop.

A THOUSAND THANK YOUS FOR YOUR LETTER

Tusind tak for dit brev, every two weeks, you would thank your father,
always the same opening that I came to recognise as I watched
over your shoulder, the same Parker Pen, the pale blue airmail paper,

Basildon Bond, and a Danish/English dictionary, for when you forgot
the Danish for English or the English for Danish, and how to express
exactly what you wanted to say, a word or phrase you could not

remember in one language that came more easily in the other – the stress
of writing this letter would eat up your mornings and afternoons,
as you flipped from one half of the dictionary to the other to impress

your father with your perfect Danish, because it was so many moons
since you had left Copenhagen, more often you knew the word or phrase
in English, but not what it was in Danish, and just as consulting the runes

can only reveal another perspective, the dictionary was a linguistic maze
that could lead to a dead end or a blindgyde, and a blindgyde to a blind
alley, or a fork which was not a gaffel that would make you reappraise

how you could spell out what it was like living this life, just how to find
a script in response to his letter, prove *a thousand thank yous* was not a bind.

SMALL TALK

after Faith Ringgold's 'Windows of the Wedding #7: Small Talk'

VVVVVVVVVVVVVVVVVVVVV
We talk in triangles
of colour – how your hope
for a clear blue sky is
congruent with my wish
to wear an orange dress.
We erect a tent of
grass and river and stitch
into diamonds the slant
facets of every day.
How harlequin we are.
Is this dress light or burnt
orange? Your waistcoat sage
or green? Conversations
of leaves and berries, half
murmured translations of
streams, mossy banks. Snippets
of repeating patterns.
From the west, a cloud of
silence needles towards
fault lines of fire, scrub and
desert where lit and burnt
orange reconcile in
parallels of meaning.
My blue touches the veins
on your wrist. Your blue swaps
to a masculine end.
Talk is gesture made strange.
Sun sets behind the trees,
shadows mouth wounds, acid

words become alkaline,
become neutralised. A
blood moon and dusk is the
quiet of doves roosting.
How was your day? Echoes
from mountains we have scaled
and descended. Discourse
reaches iced peaks, green troughs,
responds with a mirror
image. Prayer flares into
passion. Silence signs peace.
VVVVVVVVVVVVVVVVVVVVV

WOMAN

after Faith Ringgold's 'Windows of the Wedding #3: Woman'

ooooooooooooooooooooooooooooooo
Red is the silence of my lips
Yellow the crease between fingers
Blue is the roped veins on my wrist
Green is the brush of my forearm
Red is the ripeness of these lips
Pink is the tap against my nose
Yellow the shaking of fingers
Green is the graze of my forearm
Green is the scratching of my chin
Blue is the stroking of this hand
Yellow the pinching of a hair
Red is a hooked finger on chin
Green is scratching near my armpit
Yellow the flicking of my hair
Pink is the dimpling of my cheek
Red is the blood on bitten lips
Pink is the dimpling of my cheek
Red is the blood on bitten lips
Yellow the shaking of fingers
Blue is the circling of my wrist
Pink is the screw into my cheek
Yellow the crease between fingers
Green is the scratching of my chin
Blue is the stroking of this hand
Blue is the rubbing of my wrist
Yellow the flicking of my hair
Red is the ripeness of these lips
Pink is the tap against my nose
Blue is the roped veins on my wrist

Green is the brush of my forearm
Yellow the shaking of fingers
Pink is the sweet spot on my cheek
oooooooooooooooooooooooooooooooo

LIFE

after Faith Ringgold's 'Windows of the Wedding #9: Life'

✳✳✳✳✳✳✳✳✳✳✳✳✳✳✳✳✳✳
Amniotic blue, black velvet
origami purse, skin thin as
a beige (mothballed) stocking, piglet
suckling milk-come-in blues, has
one green eye on the unsucked teat,
sore nipples and the four-hour nights,
dark days drip like cooling, weak tea,
bipolar line, dividing stripe
that strips roses from the whey-faced,
then one day the smell of cut grass,
the sky is sharp with diamonds,
crawling, wobbling, *this too shall pass*,
eyes are bloodshot and circled black,
drawn face made up in the dark,
let the blue light seep through the crack
in the curtains with coffee marks,
the little fist balls up pure puce,
new as a grass blade breaking through
to claim its right to the green juice
of spring before the insect zoo
swarms, toffee dreams of sugared sleep
stick like molasses until rain
pitter-patters, storm ditches creep
with a smudge of mosquitoes, strains
of flesh-toned lullabies, jaded
jazz, and all that, valentine tat
bin-bagged, sensible soles, faded
memories of dusk before that
changeling hour, candles, fireworks,

view from the hill, lake spread below,
lure of carmine lips, midnight perks
lido backstrokes to libido,
floating at night, a moonless sky,
baby, say baby, skin-to-skin,
love, say love, salad days, cry
a river, dark womb, light gets in,
echoes turn into an image
on a screen, waves bounce back from bone,
relic found on a pilgrimage,
life, say new life, black, blue, atone.
****

SILENT MOVIE

The moon is amazing,
   but neither of them is noticing it.
The moon could be full and orange,
   a Hunter's Moon, or it could be about
to disappear behind a cloud,
   shaped like a black heart,
but they are not looking up –

the bench is centre frame,
   although it is just somewhere
for them to stop and sit.
   The bench could have a plaque
in memory of two other people
   who sat here once,
or it could be missing a slat,

graffiti scratched on by some blade,
   or it could be lichen-covered
with an empty cider bottle underneath
   resting in the damp earth.
The bench is definitely in a graveyard,
   although neither of them,
the boy nor girl, has noticed –

stopped to read the headstones.
   If a stone had one of their names,
they wouldn't notice. The girl
   is sitting on the boy's lap.
She has climbed on top of him
   and is facing him.

He shifts to accommodate her thighs
   which are heavy compared
to the thighs of a boy
   who sat on his lap
in the very same position
   just the other night. She is saying
something. He looks like
   he is listening,

but he is not really listening.
   He is thinking about that boy,
dreaming of his lips
   which he remembers and sees
more clearly than her face,
   the bench, the headstones, the moon –
how he noticed their perfect Cupid's bow.

BEFORE LIGHTS OUT

'I'll go and do the necessaries,' you say,
leaving me space to fill up the vase of myself,
and stare at my grandfather's painting of a blue vase overflowing
with poppies, daisies, and strange yellow flowers, plumes spilling
in fluffy sprays as you piss in the toilet bowl in the bathroom –
and it comes to me, their name, *goldenrod*, and how necessary
this sowing and springing up and gathering and relieving is,
and letting paint flow and piss flow, and I think of another flower,
pis-en-lit, pissy bed, wet-the-bed, all the incontinent names for dandelion,
its diuretic properties – loathed flower – so often weeded out,
remedy for cystitis, kidney stones, water retention, wiped out –
but Isaac Levitan's *Dandelions* are preserved in an earthenware vase,
yellow flowers and white clocks suspended in oil, ticking time on
mass deportations, wars, refugees fleeing, the idea a Jew should not
be painting the Russian countryside, but then the story of the curtain rising
on the underwater scene he painted for the opera, *Rusalka,*
the crescendo of applause spilling out from the theatre –
interrupted by the crash of the toilet lid that follows your stream
becoming a trickle, becoming the last few drops shaken before
you fill the doorframe, turn the light out on the vase
painted while my grandfather was living under occupation in Copenhagen
filling the vase of himself with watery blues, bleeding reds, splashy yellows –
and I swim away to sink into the dip of the mattress where our bodies
have been vases all these years filling and leaking and in sleep excreting
yellow petals on sheets, painted from sweat and urea and salts –
all our necessary toxins carried away from our underwater selves.

METAMORPHOSES: COLOURS, MARKS AND SIGNS

Silver
In sign language, silver
is a hook of little fingers
flashing into a filigree.

A christening bracelet
glints on my daughter's wrist. But look!
How quick it is an outgrown O.

Green
Walked in crocodile pairs
past artificial flowers in
a window box with acid leaves.

Once, I dug my thumb nail
in a rubber plant and sap leaked –
the shock of the real made me cry.

Pink
'Think Pink!' is a show tune
in *Funny Face* – a strategy
'gainst drudgery, the kitchen sink.

Pink petals were printed
on the pale paper of my wrist
as the kettle sang out its song.

Blue
This is how we build blue
into our lives – climb to the roof
to witness a space oddity.

Boo held onto the blue
rubber ring by her bite as I
swung her around. She left teeth marks.

Black
When Boo disappeared down
a deep rabbit hole – the horror
of loss until the dirt gave birth.

After Boo had six pups with
black spots, she was no longer
mine. She was lost to motherhood.

Gold
The church smelled of warm wood.
My ten-year-old played 'The Swan' on
her saxophone for her mormor,

The Danish love butter.
I held a buttercup under
my mother's chin – it glowed gold. Proof.

Red
Loss and warmth in the red
scarf, round my neck, she wore over
her mouth to not breathe in raw air.

The scarf still smells of her.
When my son wears it, I worry
he'll lose it, just like I lost her.

Purple
Over seventeen signs
for purple. Overripe with reds
and blues, a flickering magic.

Dusk leaked through blinds. I shut
Flower Fairies of the Trees, wished
I could flit with the bats and moths.

Rainbow
We are caught up in the
colours of souls that went before.
Dante called them *ombra* – just shades.

In hospital, aged five,
my leg in traction, an angel
came. He wore motley pyjamas.

SPORE POEM*

(after tweets between 2 Jan 2021 – 27 August 2021)

Thankful for an evening walk. Thankful for an end of an era, end of class, end of BSL exams – retakes don't count – end of summer. Thankful for someone smoking in the bushes before realising it's nettles pollinating. Thankful for rain and long and leafy corridors, for grassy beginnings in horse shit, for spiked conker cases like medieval weapons, for circles on ponds forming, intersecting, disappearing. Thankful for a prehistoric animal from fallen branches, its sunken eye and strange, sad snout. Thankful my heart is green. Thankful for a baby moorhen contemplating its own reflection, for a gorgeous orchid delivered today, for *Parallel Movement of the Hands*, a paean to possibility. Thankful my eyes itcheth. 'Night, night sweet honeysuckle, night night.' Thankful for *The Dark Horse* in my darkening garden, for the moon, peculiar in its croissant incarnation. Thankful for Selina's fierce new collection. Thankful for birds on a wire, swallows, I think. Thankful for a tame heron and a caged mushroom, for a woman making a fence with cherry, ash, and ivy ties. Thankful for a Crinkle-Crankle wall, its curves trapping the sun's warmth, encouraging the growth of fruit in alcoves.

A DIPTYCH IS NOT A DICK PIC,

although both could be considered a fragile
request for an intimate audience. The diptych,
a portable pair of carved or painted panels,
for private devotion. The Dick Pic,
a portable picture of a pair of testes and an erect –
or flaccid – penis for private devotion. Except,
recipients' reactions do vary. It hinges

on whether the Dick Pic is unsolicited. Cringes/
violation as opposed to shivers/anticipation.
The owner of a diptych chose the dual depiction
presumably. If they found a goat opposite a devil –
the medieval equivalent of cyberflashing –
instead of a white lamb tenderly staring at angels,
sod the perfect angles, the egg tempera, the shading.

SATURN DEVOURING HIS SON

painted at Quinta del Sordo (Deaf Man's Villa)

On Saturn, it is raining diamonds.
Soot falls and Goya picks up his palette.
He has a choice of four blacks: bone black,
lamp black, ivory black and red black.
A prophecy declares war on Justice.
The very thing Saturn is warned will happen — *one of his sons will
    overthrow him —*
spurs him to snatch his son, dig his fingers deep
into the boy's torso and bite off his head.
Soot is falling on Saturn and as it descends
Goya considers the reds at his disposal,
just two: vermilion and burnt sienna,
but there is no subtlety in blood — *when blood is spilled, it is noticed,
    however tiny the drop —*
when red is applied to a dark canvas,
it commands the gaze as a graze
on a child's knee commands the gaze.
This is Goya's black period. The painting
is on the wall. Lightning storms are turning
methane into soot. Soot falls on Saturn — *Saturn, god of time,
    attempts to reverse fate —*
a god gobbles his future and summons Justice.
Goya sizes up the painting on the wall.
What black will he use for the pupils?
Eyes lit with frenzy. Perhaps lamp black.
As soot falls on Saturn, it could be described
as carbon black which hardens as Saturn's will — *he fetishises fate,
    eats the meat of his flesh —*
he butchers his boy in a state of bone black
arousal. Graphic violence as soot falls

on Saturn and hardens into graphite,
falls further, plummeting new depths
to crystallise into diamond hailstones,
showering riches on Saturn, and Goya – *who paints with oils on his*
    dining room wall –
dips his brush in red black for the cavity
of Saturn's mouth. As the uncut diamonds
rain down earth-span after earth-span
into Saturn's hot core, where the heat
is hellish and the pressure for change
inescapable, they melt in a sea of carbon – *and Goya paints Saturn*
    on his knee in ivory black.

HAVE YOU SEEN A TREE FALL?

I saw a tree fall in a wood once,
as in once upon a time, as in once.
I was young and with my father

in the wood, the wood where we
walked most Sundays. All those walks
falling into each other, all those Sundays

through beech and oak and down
the side of the old quarry, up to the ridge,
the same Sunday walk, the comfort

of ritual, but this one standout moment,
separated from all the others, that closed
like a fan, into a stiff, held memory

of a Sunday walk to be considered.
That tree, like a closed ebony fan,
was dark and hard and to be considered,

because the tree became a symbol
with its own secret language, that could
upbraid me for my semiotic ignorance,

that could rap me on the head if I didn't spot
the hole, the missing sticks, the deep crack,
the way leaf was lost from the outside in.

But I was young, I understood none of this.
I stood and watched the tree fan out
and fall, take up all the space in the wood

for one rushing moment, sweeping away sky,
sweeping away the figure of my father,
sweeping every Sunday walk into once

upon a time, the way a fan drawn across
eyes means, *I am sorry,* and placed behind
the head means, *don't forget me.*

BLUE HYDRANGEA

A dead hydrangea is as intricate and lovely as one in bloom
— Toni Morrison, *Tar Baby*

The Emperor fed you eggshells,
coffee grounds and citrus peel
to turn you from pink to blue.

The Emperor did not want a girl,
a blowsy girl, common as hell,
you understand. He wanted you.

The Emperor prized your petals,
how they skirted, how they fell,
how they kaleidoscoped to view.

The Emperor at the windlass well,
turned the handle, lowered the pail,
pulled up an acidic brew.

The Emperor crooned *Water Vessel*,
poured and sang, then set sail
to search for where the bluest grew.

The Emperor was gone a spell,
earth chalked up the pH scale,
your petals blushed a pinker hue.

The Emperor sensed his quest fail,
felt his remorse swell
for neglecting the most true.

The Emperor fed you rusty nails,
white vinegar and fish scales
to turn you from pink to blue.

RUNNING AT DUSK

It has been raining, raining hard all day.
Somewhere it has rained so hard,
flood water has risen. Furniture floats
in the living room, a framed family has dived
from the sideboard into the swirling waters,
but that is somewhere, not here, here it is evening.

The all-day rain has stopped, water has given way
to fading light, yet the ground remains ribbed
like the shell of a walnut. I am running
around the park because it is dry enough to escape
televised news of floods as my arms swing
and my open hands pump air to help me along.

I think of the sign language for evening,
the shutters of the hands do not come down
in that final blinkered collapse of night;
instead, they stutter in a dance move of darkness
as if they want to wave in and wave away light,
a drawbridge with a mechanical fault.

Somewhere other hands are pumping
water that should not be inside, outside.
All these elements we want in perfect balance.
My hands pump on in their asynchronous swing
through the swelling dusk as a fiery bee hovers –
feeling for the flower of a linden tree.

HOWL

Brecean, Brittany, 11 September 2021

They told me they found two owls,
two dead owls, and they supposed
the owls must have flown down
the chimney and the owls had no way
of knowing how to fly back up
the chimney into the night sky.
They died a desiccated death
and they told me if I'd seen the owls,
I would have cried. The owls were
barn owls, beautiful and the extraordinary
thing was the weight of the owls,
incredibly and unexpectedly light.
They put the owls in a bin bag
because owls are a protected species
and this is what the town hall said
must be done and to drop off the owls
at the town hall. I wanted to know
more about the owls and asked
if they died together but no,
one owl died at one end of the loft
and the other owl not especially nearby.

FROM **HERON**

From here on,
I'm acknowledging
that not every sign
is an envoy from a kinder god
with a colloquial ascent –
the heron, in flight, over the lake,
is just a badly crafted idea of a paper aeroplane.

DEAF SKY, DANISH SAND

If clouds are like my fingers,
ever-moving, making shapes,
varying speeds, then silence
is blue sky belied by the pulse
of veins throbbing in wrists.

What chance of Danish grains
beneath my feet on this Brittany
beach carried in the longboat
of my imagination where every day,
I miss my mother's accent,
taste my husband's mother tongue.

A VALID EXCUSE

It was a beautiful day, I will tell them.
I felt myself flowering towards the feminine.
The mechanical digger dealing in dirt was a distraction
from the girl on her bike in the rainbow dress
and a helmet with a pink unicorn horn. Any beauty
would be lost in the retelling, I will tell them.
I envied the cat basking in beauty and the pregnant model
in an orange leopard skin bikini lying on the grass.
One living in the present, the other expectant.
Why pick up pen and paper on a day like this I will ask?
I will tell them – and they will understand – it was a beautiful day.

NOTES AND ACKNOWLEDGEMENTS

With gratitude to the editors of the magazines, where some of these poems first appeared. With thanks to the Torriano Meeting House poets, and to Stav Poleg, and Laura Scott for their excellent advice over the years. Thanks for the collaboration and inspiration to Deaf artists Raymond Antrobus, Ilya Kaminsky, Nadia Nadarajah, Sophie Stone, Nina Thomas, and DL Williams; and to my brilliant BSL teachers Emma Lliffe, Caroline Palmer, Antony Rabin, Andrew Stanley and Alison Wherry-Alimo. A huge thank you to all the Carcanet team for all their brilliant support. An especial thank you to Jazmine Linklater, my super-sharp editor, who helped with the shaping of this collection to realise its political vision. Thank you to John McAuliffe for judging balance and smoothing sharp edges. Thank you to Michael Schmidt for believing in this project from the beginning. Thanks to Andrew Latimer for his incredible book design. A debt of thanks is due to Dr Sarah Jackson at Nottingham Trent University for the commission that led to the collection's title poem; and to Eleanor Livingstone for commissioning 'Darning Mushroom' for StAnza 2021 in partnership with Fife Contemporary. Thank you and love always to Lottie McCrindell for her sympathetic eye cast over earlier drafts of the manuscript, and finally a huge heartfelt thanks to the Society of Authors for awarding an Authors' Foundation Grant, giving me the space and time to complete this collection.

'Researches in Electric Telephony – A Coupling' is a form invented by the poet Karen McCarthy Woolf

'Mushroom Machine' includes a haiku using *https://www. poem-generator.org.uk/haiku/*

'Sign Language of Home' was published in *Poetry Ireland Review*, Issue 135

'The House of the Interpreter' was in response to a commission by Dr Sarah Jackson for 'The Exchange', a collaboration between Crossed Lines and the Science Museum Group responding to telephony from a D/deaf and marginalised perspective. It was the genesis for a collaborative film-poem which can be seen here: https://crossedlines.co.uk/the-house-of-the-interpreter/

'Ear Trumpet, possibly used during a period of mourning, Europe, 1850-1910' was published by *Zoeglossia*, a community for poets with disabilities

'Blackbird and Beethoven' was published in *Poetry Wales*, Issue 58

'from D/diaries: Saturday morning, lying in bed, 9th February 2019' was published by *harana poetry*, Issue 3

'Call an Airborne Loved One' was published by *bath magg*, Issue 6

'#WhereIsTheInterpreter' was published by deaf blog, *Limping Chicken*, and a signed version was broadcast on *See Hear* in response to the government's failure to provide a British Sign Language interpreter for daily government briefings on the coronavirus pandemic, which was subsequently judged illegal for breaking the Equality Act 2010

'If my deaf ear were a mushroom' was published in *Butcher's Dog*, Issue 15

'Mushroom to Svamp' was published in *PN Review*, Issue 260 (47:6)

'Red Data List of Threatened British Fungi: Mainly Smuts' was published in *PN Review*, Issue 260 (47:6) and Highly Commended for the 2022 Forward Prizes for Poetry

'Cup Fungi on the Red List' was published in *Finished Creatures*, Issue 5

'Mycology Abecedarian' was published in *The Lonely Crowd*, Issue 13

'Mycelium' was published in *Brittle Star*, Issue 47

'Mushroom' was published in *The Lonely Crowd*, Issue 13

'Amanita Muscaria' was published by *perverse*, Issue 5H

'Mushroom Stones' was published in the anthology *Ecopoetry* (Broken Sleep Books)

'Alternate Reality' was published in *PN Review*, Issue 260 (47:6)

'Mycelium Lampshade' was published in *The Lonely Crowd*, Issue 13

'Darning Mushroom' appeared in an online exhibition 'Resolve to Make it New' for *Fife Contemporary* in partnership with StAnza 2021, and another version was published in *Finished Creatures*, Issue 5

'Scarlett Caterpillar Club' was published in *PN Review*, Issue 260 (47:6)

'Mushroom Machine' was published in *PN Review*, Issue 260 (47:6)

'Six Ways Mushrooms Can Change The World' was published by *The Interpreter's House*, Issue 76

'Mycology' was published by *Hencroft Hub*, Issue 1

'In Search of Cowbane Rust' was published in *PN Review*, Issue 260 (47:6)

'Watery Milkcap' was published in *Finished Creatures*, Issue 5

'Small Talk' was published by *Tentacular*, Issue 8

'Life' was published by *Tentacular*, Issue 8

'Silent Movie' was published in *The Pomegranate London*, Issue 3

'Metamorphoses: Colours, Marks and Signs' was published in *Poetry Salzburg Review 40*

'Saturn Devouring His Son' was published by *The Manchester Review*, Issue 24

'Have you seen a tree fall?' was published by *The Manchester Review*, Issue 24

'Blue Hydrangea' was published by *Bad Lilies*, Issue 7

'Running at Dusk' was published in *Poetry Birmingham Literary Journal*, Issue 3

'Howl' was published by *Atrium Poetry*

'A Valid Excuse' was published in *Ambit*, Issue 242